**NEW YORK HAS
ROMANCED ME UNLIKE
ANYTHING ELSE.**

BLAKE LIVELY

Lisa Nieschlag   Lars Wentrup

IN LOVE WITH

NEW YORK

Recipes & Stories from the City that Never Sleeps

FOOD PHOTOGRAPHY
Lisa Nieschlag

NEW YORK PHOTOGRAPHY
Joe Thomas

Hardie Grant

BOOKS

CONTENTS

STARTING THE DAY TOGETHER

Breakfast & Brunch

❤

THE LOVELIEST PARKS

Picnic, Snacks & Street Food

❤

SWEET BIG APPLE

Sweets & Cakes

Frosted Red Velvet Cake*	92
Chocolate Mousse Cake	95
Raspberry Crumble Blondies	96
Sweet Potato Tartlets	101
Key Lime Pie	102
Salted Caramel Cheesecake	105
Big Apple Hand Pies	108
Stracciatella Cupcakes	111
Double Chocolate Mud Cake*	114
Blueberry Muffins	117
Banana Bread Cashew Bars	118
Peanut Butter Donuts	121
Triple Choc Cookies	124
Cookies and Cream Ice Cream	127

♥

Sex and the City	88
Harry & Sally	106

ON CLOUD NINE

Drinks & Party Food

Negroni*	134
Shrimp Sliders	137
Chicken Curry Skewers	142
Coleslaw in a Jar	145
Chinatown Spring Rolls	148
Sake Mojitos with Ginger	151
Enchilada Cups	154
Caprese Soup Shots	159
Coated Nuts	160
Sesame Crackers with (Bell)	
Pepper Salsa	165
Cosmopolitan	166

♥

From the Rooftop	130
Sleepless in Seattle	132
Sunset time	140
The Great Gatsby	152
Westside Story	162

I LEFT MY HEART
in New York

New York may not be Paris, Rome or Venice, and the Big Apple certainly has its rough side, but despite that (or maybe because of it) it is a magnet for romantics, as the countless Hollywood classics filmed against this breath-taking backdrop testify. Just the name New York conjures up unforgettable images of famous love stories. You instantly picture the Manhattan skyline, romantic horse-drawn carriage tours in Central Park, yellow taxi cabs or a red heart projected onto the front of the Empire State Building. When you are actually there, it feels so much like being on a film set that you sometimes want to pinch yourself.

Probably the most iconic metropolis in the world, New York dazzles at any time of day, in any season. When you are bowled over by the incredible energy of this city, thrilled by its tempo, inspired by its unique joie de vivre, scents and colours, or carried away by the feeling that you are a player on what must be the most exciting open-air stage on the globe. When you come across a small green oasis in the heart of the city, discover the perfect restaurant or the most beautiful sunset, or have the opportunity to experience a tiny but inspiring cultural detail. When you seize the chance to discover another language, another cuisine, another lifestyle that is only a short subway ride away. When you enjoy meeting people from every corner of the globe who live above, below and cheek by jowl with each other. When you open your eyes and take in all that there is to see, experience and love here – then New York has you under its spell.

Join us, and be guided and beguiled –
and share our love for
New York!

When New York wakes up, you can sense the unique magic of this vibrant metropolis. The first rays of the rising sun make their way between its skyscrapers to tempt us up and out, promising a wonderful day ahead.

STARTING THE DAY TOGETHER

BREAKFAST & BRUNCH

BREAKFAST
at Tiffany's

As soon as you hear *Moon River*, you can't help but think of AUDREY HEPBURN and GEORGE PEPPARD kissing passionately in the pouring rain among New York's iconic skyscrapers. Few classic films share such an intimate connection with the city as this romantic love story, which was based on Truman Capote's novella.

Enchanting party girl Holly Golightly shares a small apartment on the Upper East Side with her cat (named simply Cat). She eats breakfast in front of the display window at *Tiffany & Co*, the upmarket jeweller, sleeps until midday and is taken out to dinner by one of her many gentlemen friends in the evening.

Paul Varjak, a young and ambitious writer who is also financially dependent on a wealthy patron, rents the apartment above Holly and is immediately fascinated by her.

A close friendship quickly develops between Holly and Paul, and she affectionately names him 'Fred' because he looks like her brother. However, she refuses to admit to any romantic feelings as she has bigger fish to fry and wants to find a rich husband.

One day, Doc Golightly, an older man and country vet, turns up on Holly's doorstep with the intention of taking her back to Texas; she had married him at the age of 13, but soon fled from the restrictions and impositions of rural life and escaped to New York.

Holly decides to stay in New York and, after a wonderful day with Paul, they spend the night together. As they are both penniless, however, she insists on going through with the wedding she has planned to a Brazilian landowner until news of her brother's death turns her life upside down. Shortly thereafter, she is arrested by the police on suspicion of having links to a powerful mafia boss. Paul collects her from jail and confesses his love for her in the cab, and they eventually embrace as they scour the streets for her lost cat.

Tiffany & Co is located on Fifth Avenue and you too can now enjoy breakfast there, at its Blue Box Café.

Holly discovers a copy of the only book Paul has ever published in the New York Public Library.

ORANGE PECAN PANCAKES

SERVES 4

FOR THE BATTER

30 g (1 oz) unsalted butter

30 g (1 oz/¼ cup) pecans

2 extra large eggs

¼ teaspoon salt

200 ml (7 fl oz/scant 1 cup) milk

175 g (6 oz/1¼ cups) plain (cake) flour

1 teaspoon baking powder

30 g (1 oz) sugar

1 packet (2 teaspoons/8 g) bourbon vanilla sugar

50 ml (1¾ fl oz/3 tablespoons) orange juice

FOR THE TOPPING

70 g (2½ oz/¾ cup) pecans

2 tablespoons sugar

pinch of salt

3 oranges

3 tablespoons honey

½ teaspoon ground cinnamon

1 teaspoon cornflour (cornstarch)

OTHER INGREDIENTS

clarified butter, for cooking

To make the batter, melt the butter and chop the pecans very finely in a food processor. Separate the eggs. Whisk the egg whites with the salt to form stiff peaks. In another bowl, whisk the egg yolks with a little of the milk. Mix the flour, pecans, baking powder and both sugars together. Stir the flour mixture, the remaining milk, and the orange juice alternately into the egg yolk mixture, using short, slow movements to prevent the batter becoming heavy. Finally, mix in the melted butter and lightly fold in the beaten egg whites. Cover the batter and let it rest for 30 minutes.

To make the topping, preheat the oven to 180°C (350°F/gas 4) and line a baking tray (pan) with baking parchment.

Roughly chop the pecans and scatter over the prepared tray. Pour 2 teaspoons of boiling water into a bowl, stir in the sugar until dissolved and then pour over the nuts, mixing until they are well coated. Caramelise in the preheated oven for approximately 10 minutes. Remove the nuts from the oven, sprinkle with a pinch of salt and allow to cool.

Halve and juice one of the oranges. Peel the remaining oranges, divide them into segments and cut into cubes. Bring the orange juice, honey and cinnamon to the boil in a small pan. Stir the cornflour into 1 tablespoon of cold water until smooth. Add to the simmering liquid and stir continuously for approximately 2 minutes until thickened. Add the cubed orange segments and keep the topping warm over a low heat.

To cook the pancakes, heat a little clarified butter in a large frying pan (skillet) over a medium heat. Cook 2–3 pancakes at a time, adding 1 large tablespoon of batter to the pan for each and frying over a medium heat for 1–2 minutes per side until golden brown, turning once. Continue until all the batter has been used, keeping the cooked pancakes warm in a low oven, at around 70°C (160°F/gas ¼).

Pile the pancakes onto a large plate and top with the orange and honey mixture and the caramelised pecans before serving.

ALMOND RUGELACH WITH APRICOTS AND PISTACHIOS

To make the dough, cut the butter into small pieces, place in a bowl with the cream cheese and egg yolk, and stir until smooth. In another bowl, mix the flour with the almonds, salt, vanilla sugar and cinnamon, then slowly knead into the butter mixture until you have a smooth dough. Shape the dough into a ball, press down to flatten it slightly, wrap in cling film (plastic wrap) and refrigerate for at least 1 hour.

To make the filling, toast the almonds briefly in a dry frying pan (skillet) until golden. For the topping, finely grind the pistachios and sugar in a food processor and spread in an even layer on the work surface. Roll out the dough over the pistachio mixture into a disk approximately 4 mm (¼ in) thick and 26–28 cm (10–11 in) in diameter, turning the dough over once or twice so it is thinly coated with the mixture on both sides. Neaten the edges.

Preheat the oven to 180°C (350°F/gas 4). Spread the apricot jam over the dough, leaving a border of about 2 cm (¾ in) round the edge and a circle of about 7 cm (3 in) in diameter uncovered in the middle. Sprinkle the toasted almonds over the jam. Use a pizza cutter to slice the disk into 16 equal wedges. Roll each wedge up, starting at the wide end and finishing at the point. Press down gently on the points to seal the rolls.

Line a baking sheet with baking parchment and arrange the rugelach on top, evenly spaced apart with the points facing down. Bake in the preheated oven for 20–24 minutes until golden brown and crisp. Transfer to a wire rack and leave to cool completely.

MAKES 16

FOR THE DOUGH

100 g (3½ oz) softened unsalted butter
75 g (2½ oz/⅓ cup) full (whole) fat cream cheese
1 large egg yolk
125 g (4 oz/1 cup) plain (all-purpose) flour
25 g (1 oz/¼ cup) ground almonds (almond meal)
pinch of salt
1 packet (2 teaspoons/8 g) bourbon vanilla sugar
¼ teaspoon ground cinnamon

FOR THE FILLING

25 g (1 oz/scant ¼ cup) chopped almonds
125 g (4 oz/generous ⅓ cup) apricot jam (jelly)

OTHER INGREDIENTS

25 g (1 oz/scant ¼ cup) pistachios
25 g (1 oz) brown sugar

SOURDOUGH BREAD

MAKES 1 LONG LOAF

FOR THE SOURDOUGH

125 g (4 oz/scant 1 cup) wholemeal
  (whole wheat) flour
125 ml (4 fl oz/½ cup) lukewarm
  water
15 g (½ oz) matured sourdough
  starter

FOR THE MAIN DOUGH

275 g (10 oz/2¼ cups) plain
  (all-purpose) flour
60 g (2 oz/⅓ cup) wholemeal
  (whole wheat) flour
1½ teaspoons salt
175 ml (6 fl oz/¾ cup) lukewarm
  water
prepared sourdough (see above)
1 teaspoon matured sourdough
  (starter)
1 tablespoon rapeseed (canola) oil

OTHER INGREDIENTS

plain (all-purpose) flour, for dusting
oval proving basket (about 25 cm/
  10 in), ideally with a cloth lining

SUGGESTED TOPPINGS

cream cheese, avocado, chilli (hot
  pepper) flakes and feta
sour cream, spring onions
  (scallions), fried mushrooms and
  bacon
olive tapenade, roasted pine nuts,
  cherry tomatoes and basil
goat's cheese, figs, rosemary and
  honey (see picture)

To make the sourdough, start the evening before by mixing the flour, water and sourdough starter together well in a bowl. Cover the bowl with cling film (plastic wrap) and let the dough prove at room temperature for about 10 hours.

To make the main dough the next morning, mix the two types of flour and salt in a food processor fitted with the dough blade. Add the lukewarm water, prepared sourdough mixture, sourdough starter and rapeseed oil.

Knead on a low speed for 8 minutes and then for a further 2 minutes on medium speed. Cover the bowl with cling film (plastic wrap) and let the dough prove for about 2½ hours.

Carefully shape the dough into an elongated loaf on a lightly floured work surface, making sure not to overwork it. Place the loaf seam-side up in a heavily floured proving basket, cover and leave to prove for 1 hour. Towards the end of the proving time, preheat the oven to 250°C (480°F/gas 9) and line a baking sheet with baking parchment.

Place the dough seam-side down on the prepared baking sheet and make three diagonal cuts across the top with a sharp knife. Do this quickly to avoid the dough collapsing. Bake immediately in the preheated oven, tipping a shot glass of cold water over the bottom of the oven as the steam from it will help give the loaf a good crust. After baking for about 10 minutes, reduce the oven temperature to 220°C (430°F/gas 8) and bake for another 25–28 minutes. Leave to cool completely on a wire rack.

Cut the loaf into slices, add toppings of your choice and serve.

EGG SANDWICHES

Preheat the oven to 85°C (185°F/gas ¼). Warm the croissants in the oven on a baking sheet lined with baking parchment.

Whisk the eggs, cheese and milk together in a bowl and season with the salt and a little pepper. Rinse the chive stems and pat dry. Snip the chives into short lengths using scissors and stir into the egg mixture.

Heat the clarified butter in a frying pan (skillet), pour in the egg mixture and stir continuously over a medium heat until the eggs are scrambled and have a creamy texture. Take care not to overcook the eggs or they will become rubbery.

Remove the croissants from the oven, cut them in half crossways and spread the bottom halves with butter. Top each half with a slice of ham, some scrambled egg and 1 tablespoon of coleslaw. Replace the top halves of the croissants and serve immediately.

SERVES 4

4 croissants
6 extra large eggs
60 g (2 oz/½ cup) grated (shredded) Cheddar
4 tablespoons milk
½ teaspoon salt
6 chive stems
1 teaspoon clarified butter
4 teaspoons softened unsalted butter
4 slices cooked ham
4 tablespoons coleslaw (see recipe page 145)
freshly ground black pepper

TUNA PRETZEL BAGELS

MAKES 8

FOR THE DOUGH

450 g (1 lb/3½ cups) plain (all-purpose) flour, plus a little more if needed

50 g (1¾ oz/⅓ cup) wholemeal (whole wheat) flour

2 teaspoons salt

10 g (⅓ oz) fresh yeast or 1 teaspoon fast-action dried yeast

300 ml (10 fl oz/1¼ cups) lukewarm water

1 teaspoon sugar

1 tablespoon rapeseed (canola) oil

FOR THE FILLING

2 × 150 g (5 oz) tins of tuna in spring water

1 yellow (bell) pepper

½ bunch of chives

100 g (3½ oz/scant ½ cup) crème fraîche

150 g (5 oz/⅔ cup) cream cheese

pinch of sugar

2 teaspoons freshly squeezed lemon juice

4 tomatoes

8 cos (romaine) lettuce leaves

salt, pepper

OTHER INGREDIENTS

flour, for dusting

100 g (3½ oz/scant ½ cup) bicarbonate of soda (baking soda)

sea salt or sesame seeds, for sprinkling

unsalted butter, for spreading

To make the dough, combine the two types of flour with the salt in a bowl. If using fresh yeast, crumble it into the water, stir in the sugar until dissolved and pour into the dry ingredients. If using dried yeast, stir it into the flour and salt before pouring in the water. Add the oil and knead into a dough. Transfer the dough to a lightly floured work surface and knead for about 6 minutes until it is smooth and elastic. If the dough seems too sticky, knead in a little more flour. Return the dough to a clean, lightly greased bowl, cover with cling film (plastic wrap) and let the dough prove in a warm place for about 2 hours until doubled in volume.

Punch the dough down with your fist, transfer it to a lightly floured work surface and divide into eight 100 g (3½ oz) pieces. Shape each piece into a log and press the ends together firmly to make rings with a hole in the middle, about 4 cm (1½ in) in diameter. Arrange the dough rings on a baking sheet lined with baking parchment, cover and leave to prove again for about 30 minutes.

Preheat the oven to 190°C (375°F/gas 5) and place an ovenproof dish of water at the bottom of the oven. Steam from the water will stop the bagels from drying out while baking and give them a good crust. Add the bicarbonate of soda to 1 litre (34 fl oz/4 cups) water in a large saucepan and bring to the boil. Reduce the heat to a simmer, drop the bagels in one at a time and boil for about 30 seconds. Lift the bagels out with a skimmer and let any water drip off them so they are dry. Return the bagels to the prepared baking sheet and immediately sprinkle them with sea salt or sesame seeds. Bake in the oven for 20–24 minutes and then remove to a wire rack to cool completely.

To make the filling, drain and flake the tuna into a bowl. Cut the pepper in half, remove the seeds and dice finely. Snip the chives into short lengths using scissors. Add the diced pepper and chives to the tuna. Mix the crème fraîche and cream cheese together and stir into the tuna mixture. Add the sugar and lemon juice, then season to taste. Remove the stalks from the tomatoes and slice, and tear the lettuce leaves into pieces. Toast the bagel and spread with butter before adding the tuna mixture, tomato slices and lettuce.

RUSSIAN CHOCOLATE COFFEE CAKE

To make the dough, mix the flour, sugar, yeast and salt together in a bowl. Mix in the eggs, milk, sour cream and butter to make a dough. Transfer the dough to a lightly floured work surface and knead for about 8 minutes until it is smooth and elastic. Add the raisins and briefly knead them in. Return the dough to a lightly greased bowl, cover with cling film (plastic wrap) and let the dough prove for about 2½ hours.

To make the filling, toast the almonds in a dry frying pan (skillet) until golden brown. Stir in the honey to quickly caramelise the almonds. Melt the chocolate and butter together over a bain-marie, stirring until smooth. Cool, then stir in the cocoa powder and caster sugar. Finally, mix in the almonds.

Line a baking sheet with baking parchment. Roll out the dough on a floured work surface to a rectangle measuring about 35 x 50 cm (14 x 20 in). Spread the chocolate mixture evenly over the dough, leaving a narrow border all around the edge. Roll up tightly and evenly from one short side, then cut the roll lengthways in half with a sharp knife. Holding one end of each half, carefully braid the two lengths together, making sure the cut sides showing the layers of dough and chocolate are always on top. Shape into a ring on the prepared baking sheet and press the ends together to seal. Cover and leave to prove for 30 minutes.

Preheat the oven to 180°C (350°F/gas 4) and bake for about 40 minutes. If the top of the cake starts to brown too quickly, cover with foil. Leave to cool completely and then sprinkle with caster sugar to serve.

MAKES 1 CAKE

FOR THE DOUGH
425 g (15 oz/scant 3½ cups) plain (all-purpose) flour
80 g (3 oz/⅓ cup) sugar
2 teaspoons fast-action dried yeast (about 5 g/¼ oz)
¼ teaspoon salt
3 large eggs
3½ tablespoons lukewarm milk
50 g (1¾ oz/¼ cup) sour cream
85 g (3 oz) softened unsalted butter
70 g (2½ oz/½ cup) raisins

FOR THE FILLING
75 g (2½ oz/½ cup) chopped almonds
1 tablespoon honey
100 g (3½ oz) dark chocolate, chopped
75 g (2½ oz) unsalted butter
3 tablespoons cocoa (unsweetened chocolate) powder
3¼ tablespoons caster (superfine) sugar

OTHER INGREDIENTS
flour, for dusting
caster (superfine) sugar, for sprinkling

GRANOLA BERRY BOWLS

SERVES 4

FOR THE GRANOLA

150 g (5 oz/1¼ cups) fine oatmeal

110 g (4 oz/generous ¾ cup)
   mixed nuts and seeds (e.g.
   sunflower seeds, chopped
   hazelnuts, sesame seeds,
   chopped almonds)

40 g (1½ oz/ ½ cup) desiccated
   coconut

20 g (¾ oz) puffed amaranth

2 tablespoons coconut oil

4½ tablespoons honey

1 packet (2 teaspoons/8 g)
   bourbon vanilla sugar

¼ teaspoon ground cinnamon

¼ teaspoon salt

FOR THE BOWL

1 vanilla pod (bean)

½ lime

500 g (1 lb 2 oz/2 cups) Greek
   yoghurt (10 per cent fat)

1 tablespoon maple syrup

125 g (4 oz/1 cup) fresh
   raspberries

125 g (4 oz/generous ¾ cup)
   fresh blueberries

250 g (9 oz/1¼ cups) fresh
   strawberries

OTHER INGREDIENTS

2 tablespoons shredded coconut

maple syrup, for drizzling (to
   taste)

To make the granola, preheat the oven to 180°C (350°F/gas 4) and line a baking tray (pan) with baking parchment. Mix the oatmeal, nuts and seeds, desiccated coconut and amaranth together in a bowl. Melt the coconut oil in a small saucepan and add the honey, vanilla sugar, cinnamon and salt, stirring until combined. Add to the dry ingredients in the bowl and stir until evenly coated.

Spread the granola over the prepared tray and gently press it flat. Bake for 15–20 minutes until golden brown, turning the granola over once with a spoon and pressing it down slightly after turning. Leave the granola to cool until it firms up slightly, then break into medium-size pieces.

To make the vanilla and lime yoghurt, slit the vanilla pod length-ways and scrape out the seeds. Juice the lime. Stir the vanilla seeds, lime juice and maple syrup into the yoghurt. Pick through the berries, washing them carefully if necessary, and pat dry. Cut the strawberries into halves or quarters.

Toast the shredded coconut in a dry frying pan (skillet). Divide the granola between four serving bowls, top with some vanilla and lime yoghurt, the berries and shredded coconut. Drizzle with maple syrup to taste and serve.

Pillow Talk

'You are my inspiration ...' whispers the Broadway composer and committed bachelor Brad Allen (ROCK HUDSON) to his many muses on the phone. The only snag is that he has to share a phone line with emancipated and resourceful interior decorator Jan Morrow (DORIS DAY), who finds Brad's flirting quite annoying as it ties up her phone connection for hours.

Brad thinks Jan is an old maid – having only spoken to her on the phone – and is surprised to see the striking young woman dancing in a cool New York bar one evening. To teach her a lesson, he pretends to be a down-to-earth Texan named Rex Stetson and turns on his

seductive charms for her – successfully, as it happens, as Jan then falls in love with him.

Her friend and long-time admirer Jonathan Forbes (TONY RANDALL) is jealous and hires a detective to investigate his unknown rival. When this turns it to be his best friend Brad Allen, whose cheesy love songs and Broadway shows he has been financing for ages, Jonathan gives him his marching orders – Brad is packed off to work on his songs in Jonathan's cabin, with no female distractions.

Brad, alias Rex, has long since convinced Jan to join him on a trip to this very place in the country, however, and the two spend a romantic evening in front of an open fire, until Jan discovers the score for 'You are my inspiration ...', a song she knows only too well, and Brad is unmasked.

Jan now wants nothing more to do with Brad, so in order to see her again he hires her to decorate his apartment, which has been fitted out with a few bachelor-pad modifications. When Jan discovers these, she embarks on her own plan of revenge, transforming his home into an unspeakably tasteless love den. At this, Brad sweeps up Jan (still in her pyjamas) and carries her across Manhattan to propose to her in his apartment.

The view of the Chrysler Building from Jonathan's office is breathtaking, although most of the film was shot in a studio.

FRENCH TOAST FILLED WITH AVOCADO AND BACON

Fry the bacon in batches in a dry frying pan (skillet) over a medium heat for about 5 minutes until crispy. Drain on paper towel. Wash the tomato, remove the stalk and core and cut the flesh into small cubes. Rinse the chives, pat dry and snip into short lengths using scissors. Finely grate the Parmesan.

To make the guacamole filling, halve the avocados, remove the stones and scoop out the flesh into a bowl. Halve the lime and squeeze the juice into the bowl. Add the olive oil and mash the avocado mixture with a fork (or you can use a hand-held blender). Mix in the diced tomato and chives, and season the guacamole to taste with salt and cayenne pepper.

Lay the slices of toast on the work surface and spread four of them with a little guacamole. Top each slice with 2 rashers of bacon and sprinkle with the Parmesan. Spread cream cheese over the remaining slices and lay them on top, cheese side down, pressing down gently.

Whisk the eggs with the milk and cream in a large bowl and season with salt and cayenne pepper. Dip the French toast in the egg mixture, turning them over once so the bread is well coated on both sides, and let the excess drip back into the bowl. Fry the French toast in clarified butter in batches in a griddle pan over a medium heat for 3–4 minutes on each side until golden brown. Cut in half diagonally and serve immediately.

SERVES 4

8 bacon rashers (approx. 100 g/3 ½ oz)
1 large tomato
5 chive stems
30 g (1 oz) Parmesan
2 ripe avocados
1 lime
1 tablespoon olive oil
8 large slices of toast
100 g (3½ oz/ ½ cup) cream cheese
100 ml (3½ fl oz/scant ½ cup) milk
50 ml (1¾ fl oz/3 tablespoons) whipped cream
salt
cayenne pepper

OTHER INGREDIENTS
clarified butter, for cooking

HEARTY BREAKFAST BOWLS

SERVES 4

600 g (1 lb 5 oz) waxy potatoes

¾ teaspoon salt

½ teaspoon sweet paprika

¼ teaspoon freshly grated
  nutmeg

pinch of freshly ground black
  pepper

2 tablespoons rapeseed (canola)
  oil

8 chive stems

4 sprigs of parsley

250 g (9 oz) mushrooms

80 g (3 oz) oak leaf lettuce

½ teaspoon honey

1 tablespoon white balsamic
  vinegar

3 tablespoons olive oil

8 bacon rashers (approx. 100 g/
  3½ oz)

1 teaspoon clarified butter

6 tablespoons white wine
  vinegar

4 eggs

OTHER INGREDIENTS

4 slices sourdough bread
  (see recipe page 18)

1 teaspoon clarified butter

4 tablespoons aioli (see recipe
  page 137)

Preheat the oven to 220°C (430°F/gas 8). Wash the potatoes thoroughly and cut into quarters lengthways. Mix the salt, paprika, nutmeg, pepper and rapeseed oil in a bowl. Arrange the potato quarters on a baking tray (pan) lined with baking parchment, brush the oil and spice mixture all over them and bake in the preheated oven for about 30 minutes until the potatoes are golden brown and crispy, making sure they do not burn.

While the potatoes are baking, rinse the herbs and pat dry. Snip the chives into short lengths using scissors. Strip the parsley leaves off the stalks and chop the leaves. Clean the mushrooms, pat dry and halve or quarter, depending on the size. Wash the lettuce, spin dry and tear into bite-size pieces. Stir the honey into the balsamic vinegar and season to taste with salt and pepper. Slowly whisk in the olive oil until emulsified. Toss the lettuce with the dressing. Fry the bacon in a dry frying pan (skillet) until crispy and drain on some paper towel. In the same pan, fry the mushrooms in the bacon fat and clarified butter for about 5 minutes. Season with half the chopped parsley, salt and pepper.

To poach the eggs, bring about 2 litres (70 fl oz/8 cups pints) water and 2 tablespoons of the vinegar to the boil in a large saucepan, then reduce the heat so the water is simmering. Divide the remaining vinegar between four cups and carefully crack an egg into each one, taking care not to break the yolks. Swirl the water with a large spoon, slide the eggs into the water one at a time and poach for about 4 minutes over a low to medium heat. Drain the eggs with a skimmer and sprinkle with the chives.

Meanwhile, toast the bread slices with clarified butter in a griddle pan until golden. Divide the potatoes between serving bowls and sprinkle with the remaining parsley. Add the bacon, mushrooms, lettuce, eggs and slices of bread alongside. Spoon some aioli into each bowl and serve immediately.

Good Morning
NEW YORK

It may be known as the city that never sleeps, but few things beat waking up on a clear, sunny morning in New York and feeling that the world is your oyster. Dive in, either on the subway or via the giant main concourse of Grand Central Station with its celestial ceiling mural complete with zodiac signs (and the dark spot left to show just how sooty the ceiling was before it was restored!), and take a coffee to go and a pastrami sandwich, or maybe a bagel with cream cheese and lox. Now you're ready for anything!

CRANBERRY BREAKFAST BREAD

Preheat the oven to 175°C (340°F/gas 3). Generously butter a loaf tin (pan), 25 cm (10 in) long, and sprinkle granola over the base. Mix the flour, ground almonds, baking powder, salt and sugar in a mixing bowl. Cut the butter into small pieces and rub it into the dry ingredients with your fingertips, then stir in the maple syrup, yoghurt, eggs and milk and mix until you have a smooth batter.

Chop the cranberries finely. Toast the chopped almonds in a dry frying pan (skillet) until golden. Wash the half lemon in warm water, pat dry and finely grate the zest. Fold the cranberries, almonds and lemon zest into the batter, scrape it into the tin and smooth the top. Bake in the oven in 60–70 minutes until golden brown and a skewer inserted into the middle of the bread comes out clean. If the top starts to brown too quickly, cover loosely with foil for the last third of the baking time.

Cool the baked loaf in the tin for 20 minutes, then carefully turn it out onto a wire rack and leave to cool completely before slicing.

MAKES 1 LOAF

250 g (9 oz/2 cups) plain
   (all-purpose) flour
50 g (1¾ oz/generous ⅓ cup)
   ground almonds (almond meal)
2 teaspoons baking powder
¼ teaspoon salt
100 g (3½ oz/½ cup) sugar
125 g (4 oz) softened unsalted
   butter
3 tablespoons maple syrup
175 g (6 oz/scant ¾ cup) Greek
   yoghurt
4 large eggs
3 tablespoons milk
100 g (3½ oz/¾ cup) dried
   cranberries
50 g (1¾ oz/⅓ cup) chopped
   almonds
½ organic lemon

OTHER INGREDIENTS

unsalted butter, for greasing the
   loaf tin (pan)
4 tablespoons granola (see recipe
   page 28), or oatmeal

COFFEE SMOOTHIES

MAKES 2 LARGE DRINKS

2 ripe bananas

1–2 tablespoons flaked almonds

½ vanilla pod (bean)

½ tin of coconut milk
(about 200 ml/7 fl oz/scant
1 cup)

250 ml (8½ fl oz/1 cup) freshly
brewed strong coffee, cooled

2 tablespoons ground almonds
(almond meal)

2–3 tablespoons honey, plus
extra to taste

½ teaspoon ground cinnamon

Peel the bananas and cut into slices. Put the slices on a plate and freeze them for at least 45 minutes.

Meanwhile, toast the flaked almonds in a dry frying pan (skillet) until golden. Split open the vanilla pod and scrape out the seeds. Open the tin of coconut milk without shaking it, remove 2–3 tablespoons of the solid cream that has settled at the top, stir until smooth and reserve. Pour 175 ml (6 fl oz/ ¾ cup) of the coconut water at the bottom into a blender.

Add the cooled coffee, ground almonds, honey, cinnamon, frozen banana slices and vanilla seeds to the coconut water and blend until smooth and creamy. Add extra honey to taste if needed. Pour the smoothie into two tall glasses, add a couple of spoon-fuls of the coconut cream to each, then sprinkle with the flaked almonds and serve.

VANILLA, CASHEW AND STRAWBERRY DRINKS

Soak the cashews in cold water for at least 2 hours. Drain through a sieve (fine-mesh strainer), rinse under cold water and tip into a food processor. Add 450 ml (15 fl oz/scant 1¾ cups) cold water.

Peel the banana and chop roughly into small pieces. Split open the vanilla pod and scrape out the seeds. Add the banana, vanilla seeds, maple syrup and salt to the food processor and pulse on high speed for several minutes until smooth. Pass through a sieve into a jug and chill for at least 30 minutes.

Meanwhile, wash the strawberries and remove the hulls. Peel and segment the oranges. Wash the food processor and add the straw-berries, oranges and maple syrup. Process until smooth (or purée in a tall container using a hand-held blender), adding a little cold water if the mixture is too thick. Pass through a sieve.

Half-fill four glasses with the vanilla and cashew mixture. Pour the strawberry and orange mixture on top, taking care not to mix the two layers too much. Serve immediately.

MAKES 4 DRINKS

125 g (4 oz/generous ¾ cup) cashews
1 large, ripe banana (about 200 g/7 oz)
1 vanilla pod (bean)
2 teaspoons maple syrup
pinch of salt

OTHER INGREDIENTS
250 g (9 oz/1¼ cups) fresh strawberries
2 large oranges
2 teaspoons maple syrup

Even though New York is a vibrant city known for its dizzyingly tall skyscrapers, there are also many beautiful parks where you can get away from the hustle and bustle to relax and unwind.

THE LOVELIEST PARKS

PICNICS, SNACKS & STREET FOOD

Stroll through
CENTRAL PARK

Why does everyone just adore *Central Park*? Perhaps because it makes us feel (and behave) like children again as we ride on the carousel, glide around the skating rink, or pilot a radio-controlled boat on the pond. Maybe it's a visit to the small zoo to see the penguins, which have become bona fide stars in their own right, thanks to the children's book *And Tango Makes Three*. In this memorable book, a male penguin sits on an egg and 'adopts' the chick that hatches, making New York symbolic of modern, single-sex partnerships.

The culinary delights on offer are equally memorable, from hot dogs and giant, pillowy pretzels, to soft ice cream and caramelised peanuts, all of which are sold by vendors from small carts. Alternatively, ask for a fancy picnic basket at *Dean & Deluca* or *Zabar's*, a Jewish deli which has become an institution on the Upper West Side, spread out a blanket on the grass or on one of the rocks that are a feature in the park, and watch the world go by.

The same applies, of course, to the many dark green benches, some of which bear moving plaques commemorating loved ones who have passed on. The most famous memorial in the park is the Imagine mosaic in the heart of *Strawberry Fields*, dedicated by Yoko Ono to the memory of

John Lennon, who was shot in front of the *Dakota apartment* building directly opposite one of the gates of *Central Park*.

New Yorkers use *Central Park* as a sports field, playground, promenade and public stage. You can enjoy evenings around the Shakespeare statue in the twilight, dancing the tango or watching others perform it, closely entwined. The best performances of Shakespeare's plays take place at the *Delacorte Theater*, where people once turned up at 6 a.m. with blankets and picnic baskets to ensure their place at the front of the queue for free tickets. Nowadays there is an online lottery for the coveted seats. Enjoying a performance as night falls around you is a particularly romantic experience, but under other circumstances it is best to avoid the park at night. In daylight hours, a

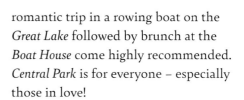

romantic trip in a rowing boat on the *Great Lake* followed by brunch at the *Boat House* come highly recommended. *Central Park* is for everyone – especially those in love!

Made in 1967 and starring JANE FONDA and ROBERT REDFORD, the film *Barefoot in the Park* made *Washington Square Park* the epitome of young love with all its daily trials and tribulations. You will still see plenty of NYU students here, strolling and relaxing, hand in hand.

DELI PASTA SALAD

SERVES 4–6

FOR THE SALAD

300 g (10½ oz/3⅓ cups) farfalle

40 g (1½ oz/¼ cup) pine nuts

1 courgette (zucchini)

1 shallot

olive oil, for frying

80 g (3 oz) pancetta

125 g (4 oz/scant 1 cup) cherry
   tomatoes

1 yellow or orange (bell) pepper

80 g (3 oz/½ cup) sundried
   tomatoes in oil (from a jar,
   drained weight)

50 g (1¾ oz/generous ⅓ cup)
   pitted black olives

½ bunch of basil

250 g (9 oz) mozzarella (125 g/
   4 oz drained weight)

salt

FOR THE DRESSING

60 ml (2 fl oz/¼ cup) light
   balsamic vinegar, plus more
   as needed

150 ml (5 fl oz/scant ⅔ cup)
   olive oil, plus more as needed

½ teaspoon dried oregano

½ teaspoon dried thyme

salt, pepper and sugar, to taste

50 g (1¾ oz) Parmesan

To make the salad, cook the farfalle in boiling salted water according to the instructions on the packet until al dente. Drain, rinse under cold water and leave for the excess water to evaporate. Toast the pine nuts in a dry frying pan (skillet) until golden.

Wash the courgette, cut in half lengthways and then into slices. Peel the shallot and slice into rings. Heat the olive oil in the frying pan and fry the courgette and shallot for a few minutes before removing and setting aside. Cut the pancetta into small cubes and fry in the same pan until crisp.

Wash the cherry tomatoes, remove the stalks and cut in half or into quarters. Wash the pepper, cut it in half, remove the seeds and core, and cut into small cubes. Chop the dried tomatoes into small pieces, drain the olives and cut into rings. Rinse the basil, pat dry and strip the leaves off the stalks. Drain the mozzarella and cut or tear into small pieces. Mix all the prepared ingredients together in a large bowl.

To make the dressing, stir all the ingredients together except for the Parmesan and season to taste with salt, pepper and sugar. Grate the Parmesan very finely and stir into the dressing, then toss with the pasta salad. Leave to stand for at least 2 hours so the pasta can absorb the dressing, and then season again with vinegar, oil, salt and pepper.

PIZZA CALZONE

To make the dough, mix the flour, salt and yeast in a bowl and make a hollow in the middle. Pour in the water and oil and mix everything together. Knead the dough on a floured work surface for about 7 minutes until smooth and elastic. Return to the bowl, cover with cling film (plastic wrap) and let the dough prove for about 2 hours until it has doubled in volume.

To make the sauce, peel the onion and garlic and chop finely. Heat the oil in a large saucepan and sweat the onion over a medium heat for a few minutes. Add the garlic, fry briefly, then stir in the tomato purée. Stir in both types of tomatoes and the red wine. Add the bay leaf, bring the sauce to the boil and leave to simmer uncovered over a low heat for about 1 hour, stirring occasionally. Season generously with the herbs, salt, pepper and sugar. Remove the bay leaf.

To make the filling, toast the pine nuts in a dry frying pan (skillet) until golden. Remove from the heat. Clean the mushrooms by wiping them with a clean dish towel and cut into quarters or eighths. Heat the oil in the same frying pan and fry the mushrooms for 5 minutes, then season with the thyme and salt and pepper to taste. Finely dice the mozzarella and slice the olives. Cut the prosciutto into fine strips.

Preheat the oven to 250°C (480°F/gas 9) and line two baking sheets with baking parchment. Divide the dough into four equal-size pieces, each weighing about 190–200 g (6½–7 oz). Roll out two pieces of the dough on a floured work surface into disks about 5 mm (¼ in) thick and 20 cm (8 in) in diameter, and lift onto one of the prepared baking sheets. Spread 2 tablespoons of sauce on one half of each disk, leaving a border around the edge, and spoon some filling over the sauce. Carefully fold the other half of the dough over to cover the filling (the dough shouldn't be too thin or it will tear and the filling will leak out). Fold the edge of the lower half of the dough back over the lip of the top half and press down firmly with a fork to seal. Bake the calzone in the preheated oven for about 15 minutes until golden brown and crispy. Repeat with the remaining dough and filling to make four calzone.

SERVES 4

FOR THE DOUGH
480 g (1 lb 1 oz/scant 4 cups) plain (all-purpose) flour, plus extra for dusting
1 teaspoon salt
2 teaspoons fast-action dried yeast (about 7 g/¼ oz)
250 ml (8½ fl oz/1 cup) lukewarm water
75 ml (2½ fl oz/5 tablespoons) olive oil

FOR THE SAUCE
1 onion
1 garlic clove
1 tablespoon olive oil
1 tablespoon tomato purée (paste)
400 g (14 oz) tin of plum tomatoes
250 g (9 oz) chopped fresh tomatoes
50 ml (1¾ fl oz/3 tablespoons) dry red wine (or red grape juice)
1 bay leaf
1 teaspoon dried oregano
1 teaspoon dried thyme
salt, pepper and sugar

FOR THE FILLING
30 g (1 oz/scant ¼ cup) pine nuts
300 g (10½ oz) small mushrooms
1 tablespoon olive oil
½ teaspoon dried thyme
250 g (9 oz) mozzarella (125 g/4 oz drained weight)
50 g (1¾ oz/generous ⅓ cup) pitted black olives
50 g (1¾ oz) prosciutto
salt, pepper

CHICKEN THE HALAL GUYS' WAY*

SERVES 4

FOR THE CHICKEN

4 organic chicken thighs,
  bone in, about 500 g (1 lb 2 oz)
2 limes
3 garlic cloves
1 teaspoon honey
½ teaspoon sweet paprika
¼ teaspoon ground cumin
¼ teaspoon ground coriander
75 ml (2½ fl oz/5 tablespoons)
  olive oil
1 tablespoon Greek yoghurt
2 tablespoons rapeseed (canola)
  oil
salt, pepper

FOR THE RICE

125 g (4 oz/scant ⅔ cup) basmati
  rice
250 ml (8½ fl oz/1 cup) chicken
  stock
1 teaspoon olive oil
1 teaspoon ground turmeric
¼ teaspoon ground cumin

FOR THE YOGHURT SAUCE

100 g (3½ oz/generous ⅓ cup)
  mayonnaise
150 g (5 oz/scant ⅔ cup)
  Greek yoghurt
½ lime
¼ bunch of flat-leaf parsley
1 teaspoon white wine vinegar
2 teaspoons Sriracha sauce
salt, pepper

OTHER INGREDIENTS

¼ iceberg lettuce
60 g (2 oz) sundried tomatoes
  in oil (from a jar, drained weight)
125 g (4 oz/scant 1 cup) cherry
  tomatoes
50 g (1¾ oz/generous ⅓ cup)
  pitted olives

Remove the skin and any fat from the chicken thighs, rinse and pat dry. Halve the limes and squeeze the juice. Peel the garlic. Using a hand-held blender, purée the lime juice, garlic, honey, spices, olive oil, yoghurt, salt and a dash of pepper together in a mixing bowl, and set aside 4 tablespoons. Toss the chicken thighs with the remaining marinade in a shallow dish until well coated, cover and refrigerate for about 2 hours.

Heat the rapeseed oil in a large frying pan (skillet) and fry the underside of the chicken thighs (in batches, if necessary) over a medium to high heat for 5–7 minutes until golden brown. Reduce the heat, turn the thighs over, cover and fry for 7–10 minutes until golden brown. The chicken thighs should be cooked through but still tender and juicy. Leave to rest on a chopping (cutting) board for about 5 minutes, then shred the meat with two forks.

Rinse the rice in a sieve (fine-mesh strainer) under cold water and drain. Simmer gently in the chicken stock in a covered saucepan for about 20 minutes until al dente. Season with the olive oil, turmeric and cumin.

Meanwhile, make the sauce. Stir the mayonnaise into the yoghurt and juice the half lime. Rinse the parsley, pat dry, strip the leaves off the stalks and chop finely. Stir the lime juice, parsley, vinegar and Sriracha sauce into the yoghurt mixture and season to taste with salt and pepper.

Wash the lettuce, spin dry and shred finely. Slice the sundried tomatoes into strips. Wash the cherry tomatoes, remove the stalks and cut in half or into quarters. Slice the olives into rings. Stir the chicken into the reserved marinade and reheat in a saucepan. Spoon the rice onto serving plates and arrange the chicken, lettuce, tomatoes and olives on top. Serve immediately with the yoghurt sauce spooned and drizzled over.

*In 1990, the Halal Guys were the first mini food truck to serve halal meat in New York. They now operate several food trucks in the city and are expanding worldwide.

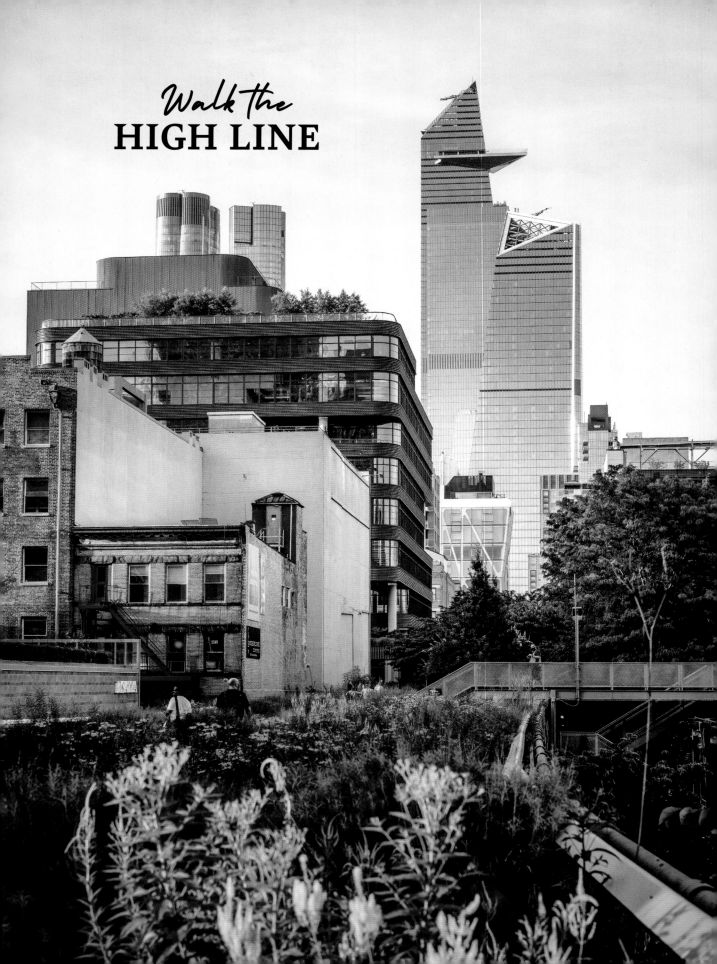

Walk the
HIGH LINE

Since 2009, the *High Line* has proved extremely popular with tourists and New Yorkers alike, with the last stretch being opened in 2019. You can now stroll along 2.33 km (1½ miles) of what was once a freight rail spur and enjoy a unique perspective of the city from the vantage point of an urban garden landscape. Pedestrian zones are almost unknown in New York but here you are raised up above the traffic and can admire cutting-edge architecture to your right and left while still being deep in the heart of the metropolis. After exploring *Chelsea*, choose an inviting bench in a green oasis to chill out and picnic.

The city's latest spectacular park project awaits near the southern tip of the *High Line* where at 10,000 square metres (2½ acres), *Little Island* is anything but little – a futuristic forest on stilts in the *Hudson River*.

Favourite WATERFRONT SPOTS

For decades, car-obsessed New York city planners have largely ignored the city's waterfronts, but things are now changing and stretches along the Hudson and East Rivers are increasingly being redeveloped so that people can enjoy a stroll, a jog or a bike ride by the water. The benches of *Gantry Plaza State Park* and *Battery Park*, for example, offer perfect vantage points from which to marvel at the majestic skylines of *Manhattan* and *New Jersey*, respectively, across the water.

CRÊPES-STYLE MANICOTTI*

To make the crêpes, melt the butter and mix the flour, salt and sugar together. Whisk the eggs with a little of the mineral water in a mixing bowl, then quickly whisk in the flour, alternately with the remaining mineral water, until you have a smooth batter. Mix in the melted butter, cover and leave to stand for 30 minutes.

Meanwhile, make the filling. Peel and finely chop the onion. Peel the carrot and cut into small cubes. Wash the celery and cut into small cubes as well. Heat the oil in a deep frying pan (skillet) and sweat the onions until softened, then add the carrot and celery and fry for 5 minutes. Add the minced beef and fry until browned, breaking up any lumps of meat with a spoon. Deglaze with the stock and simmer uncovered for about 5 minutes until the liquid has been absorbed. Rinse the parsley, pat dry, strip the leaves off the stalks and chop finely. Take the pan off the heat, stir in the parsley and season to taste with salt and pepper.

Preheat the oven to 190°C (375°F/gas 5). To cook the crêpes, heat a little oil in a frying pan, about 22 cm (9 in) in diameter, add a ladleful of the batter and spread it in a thin layer. Cook over a medium heat for 1–2 minutes on each side, turning once. Repeat using the remaining batter to make eight to ten crêpes.

To make the sauce, stir all the ingredients together and season generously with salt and pepper. Pour half the tomato sauce into an ovenproof dish, measuring about 20 x 27 cm (8 x 11 in) to cover the base. Spoon 2–3 tablespoons of the filling in a line over the lower half of each crêpe and roll up. Place the rolls, seam-side down, in the dish and pour the remaining sauce on top. Sprinkle over the mozzarella and bake in the preheated oven for 25–30 minutes.

Manicotti are very large pasta tubes that are filled and baked in a sauce. We have followed the Bevacqua family's recipe at the Reservoir Tavern and replaced the pasta with crêpes. The results are simply out of this world!

SERVES 4

FOR THE CRÊPES
25 g (1 oz) unsalted butter
150 g (5 oz/1¼ cups) plain (cake) flour
pinch of salt
pinch of sugar
3 eggs
350 ml (12 fl oz/1½ cups) sparkling mineral water

FOR THE FILLING
1 onion
1 carrot
1 celery stalk
1 tablespoon rapeseed (canola) oil, plus extra for cooking
400 g (14 oz) minced (ground) beef
3 tablespoons vegetable stock
½ bunch of parsley
salt, pepper

FOR THE SAUCE
400 g (14 oz) tin of chopped tomatoes
3 tablespoons vegetable stock
1 tablespoon balsamic vinegar
1 teaspoon brown sugar
1 teaspoon dried oregano
salt, pepper

OTHER INGREDIENTS
125 g (4 oz/scant 1 cup) grated (shredded) mozzarella

THE LOVELIST PARKS *Picnic, Snacks & Street Food*

HOTDOGS
WITH PICKLE RELISH

MAKES 6

FOR THE BUNS
20 g (¾ oz) unsalted butter
275 g (10 oz/2¼ cups) plain
  (all-purpose) flour
1 teaspoons fast-action
  dried yeast
½ teaspoon salt
15 g (½ oz) sugar
140 ml (5 fl oz/scant ⅔ cup)
  lukewarm milk
1 teaspoon honey
1 egg yolk

FOR THE PICKLE RELISH
330 g (11½ oz) jar of cornichons
  (190 g/7 oz drained weight)
1 shallot
2 teaspoons salt
50 g (1¾ oz/scant ¼ cup) sugar
1½ teaspoons mustard seeds

OTHER INGREDIENTS
flour, for dusting
6 hot dog sausages
6 chive stems
6 teaspoons tomato ketchup
6 teaspoons mustard
6 teaspoons remoulade sauce
6 tablespoons fried onions

Start making the dough for the buns the night before. Melt the butter in a small saucepan. Stir the flour, yeast, salt and sugar together in a mixing bowl. Add the milk, honey, egg yolk and butter and mix to make a dough. Knead for about 8 minutes until the dough is smooth and elastic. Cover with cling film (plastic wrap) and leave to prove for about 1 hour. Cover and refrigerate overnight. The next morning, knock the dough down, knead it briefly until smooth, then leave to prove again at room temperature for 1 hour.

While the dough is proving, make the pickle relish. Drain the cornichons, reserving about 75 ml (2½ fl oz/5 tablespoons) of the pickling brine. Cut the cornichons into small cubes. Peel the shallot and chop into pieces of the same size. Mix the cornichons and shallot in a small bowl, sprinkle with the salt and leave for 1 hour. Drain in a sieve (fine-mesh strainer).

Divide the dough into six equal pieces (each weighing about 80 g/3 oz). On a lightly floured work surface, roll the pieces first into balls and then into long sausage shapes. Place on a baking sheet lined with baking parchment, cover with cling film and leave the buns to prove for an additional 30 minutes.

Mix the reserved cornichon brine, sugar and mustard seeds in a small saucepan and briefly bring to the boil. Add the diced cornichons and shallot and cook over a low to medium heat for about 15 minutes, stirring frequently. Leave to cool.

Preheat the oven to 190°C (375°F/gas 5). Brush the buns with water and bake in the preheated oven for 20–25 minutes until golden brown. Cool on a wire rack. Heat the hot dog sausages in a saucepan of water. Rinse the chives, pat dry and snip into short lengths using scissors. Split open the buns lengthways, spread with some pickle relish and top with the hot dog sausages. Garnish each with 1 teaspoon of tomato ketchup, mustard and remoulade. Sprinkle with the fried onions and chives and serve immediately.

PASTRAMI SANDWICH

To make the sandwiches, preheat the oven to 75°C (170°F/gas ¼). Place the pastrami in a small roasting tin (pan) or casserole dish with a lid (Dutch oven) and pour over the stock, which should come about 1.5 cm (½ in) up the sides of the meat. Cover and heat up the meat in the oven for about 45 minutes.

Meanwhile, make the coleslaw. Wash the cabbage and shred it very finely. Place in a bowl with the salt and toss the cabbage vigorously with your hands until it softens slightly. Peel and finely grate (shred) the carrot, ideally using a mandolin. Peel the shallot, cut in half and slice into thin rings. Mix these with the cabbage and stir in the mayonnaise, yoghurt, mustard and creamed horseradish. Season to taste with lemon juice, salt, pepper and sugar, and mix well.

To make the dressing, stir all the ingredients together and season with pepper. Slice the gherkins thinly lengthways and toast the bread. Remove the meat from the oven, drain and slice as thinly as possible on a chopping (cutting) board.

Spread the dressing over the toasted bread, then top half the slices with coleslaw and plenty of pastrami and gherkin slices. Place the remaining slices of bread on top and press down lightly. Cut the sandwiches in half and serve immediately.

MAKES 4

FOR THE SANDWICHES
450 g (1 lb) pastrami in one piece (available online, from a delicatessen or a well-stocked butcher, ordering in advance if necessary)
about 400 ml (13 fl oz/generous 1½ cups) beef stock
8 small gherkins
8 slices Sourdough Bread (see recipe on page 18)

FOR THE COLESLAW
200 g (7 oz) white cabbage
½ teaspoon salt
1 carrot
1 shallot
75 g (2½ oz/5 tablespoons) mayonnaise
2½ tablespoons yoghurt (3.5 per cent fat)
1 teaspoon medium-hot mustard
1 teaspoon creamed horseradish
a little freshly squeezed lemon juice
freshly ground black pepper
sugar

FOR THE DRESSING
90 g (3¼ oz/6 tablespoons) mayonnaise
2 tablespoons medium-hot mustard
1 tablespoon honey
freshly ground black pepper

RAMEN

SERVES 4

1.5 litres (51 fl oz/6⅓ cups)
   chicken stock
2 eggs
2 carrots
1 baby pak choi (bok choi)
2 spring onions (scallions)
60 g (2 oz) pickled ginger
150 g (5 oz) thinly sliced,
   pre-cooked roast pork
   (from the butcher)
600 g (1 lb 5 oz) pre-cooked,
   vacuum-packed ramen
   noodles (from Asian food
   stores)
50 g (1¾ oz/3 tablespoons) light
   miso paste
50 ml (1¾ fl oz/3 tablespoons)
   mirin (sweet rice wine)
1½ tablespoons sake
   (Japanese rice wine)

OTHER INGREDIENTS
chilli oil to taste, for drizzling

Bring the chicken stock to the boil in a wide saucepan. Boil the stock over a medium to high heat, with the pan uncovered, for about 20 minutes until reduced to about 1 litre (34 fl oz/4 cups). While the stock is reducing, cook the eggs in a small pan of boiling water for about 6 minutes; the yolks should still be slightly runny. Drain, rinse the eggs under cold water, peel and halve lengthways.

Peel the carrots and cut into julienne strips using a mandolin. Wash the pak choi, shred finely and spin dry. Wash the spring onions and slice diagonally. Drain the ginger, shred finely, and cut the roast pork into strips. Cook the ramen noodles according to the instructions on the packet, drain in a sieve (fine-mesh strainer), then rinse under cold water and drain again.

Stir the miso paste, mirin and sake into the hot stock. Divide the ramen noodles between four serving bowls and ladle over the stock. Arrange the carrots, pak choi, spring onions, ginger, roast pork and egg halves on top. Drizzle the ramen soup with chilli oil to taste and serve immediately.

ASIAN NOODLE BOXES

Cook the noodles according to the instructions on the packet until al dente. Drain in a sieve (fine-mesh strainer), rinse under cold water and leave to drain again. Peel the onion, garlic and ginger. Quarter the onion and slice lengthways. Mince the garlic and ginger. Rinse the spring onions and slice diagonally, reserving a handful of the slices from the green tops as a garnish. Rinse the sugar snap peas and cut in half. Wash the pepper, cut it in half, remove the seeds and core and slice finely. Rinse the beansprouts in a sieve and leave to drain. Whisk the eggs together in a small bowl.

Heat half the oil in a wok or large frying pan (skillet), pour in the eggs and stir briefly but continuously over a medium to high heat until the eggs start to set. Add the remaining oil and all the prepared ingredients, except the noodles and beansprouts. Cook for about 5 minutes, stirring occasionally. Deglaze with the stock and briefly bring to the boil. Stir in the noodles, beansprouts, soy sauce, chilli sauce and hoisin, and stir-fry for about 3 minutes.

Meanwhile, finely chop the peanuts and juice the lime. Stir the peanuts and lime juice into the noodles, spoon onto serving dishes (or into boxes), garnish with the reserved spring onion slices and fried onions, and serve immediately.

MAKES 4 PORTIONS

300 g (10½ oz) Asian instant
 noodles, e.g. mie (wheat)
 noodles
1 small red onion
1 garlic clove
1 piece of fresh ginger (about
 2 cm/¾ in)
2 spring onions (scallions)
80 g (3 oz) sugar snap peas
1 red (bell) pepper
80 g (3 oz) beansprouts (from a
 jar, drained weight)
2 extra large eggs
50 ml (1¾ fl oz/3 tablespoons)
 peanut oil
125 ml (4 fl oz/ ½ cup) vegetable
 stock
75 ml (2½ fl oz/5 tablespoons)
 soy sauce
2 tablespoons sweet chilli sauce
1 tablespoon hoisin sauce

OTHER INGREDIENTS
50 g (1¾ oz/ ⅓ cup) roasted,
 salted peanuts
1 lime
4 teaspoons fried onions

TERIYAKI BEEF BURGERS

MAKES 4

500 g (1 lb 2 oz) rump steak
100 ml (3½ fl oz/scant ½ cup)
  teriyaki sauce
2 small spring onions (scallions)
1 red (bell) pepper
4 Chinese leaves (Napa
  cabbage)
2 tablespoons sesame seeds
4 baguette rolls
unsalted butter, for spreading
2 tablespoons sesame oil
sweet chilli sauce, for spreading

Trim any sinew or fat from the rump steak and slice into strips, about 2 cm (¾ in) wide and 4 cm (1½ in) long. Mix with the teriyaki sauce in a shallow dish. Cover and leave to marinate in the refrigerator for at least 1 hour.

Meanwhile, rinse the spring onions, slice thinly on the diagonal and separate into rings. Wash the pepper, cut it in half, remove the seeds and core and cut into small cubes. Wash the Chinese leaves and pat dry. Briefly toast the sesame seeds in a dry frying pan (skillet).

Split the baguette rolls in half. Spread the cut sides with a little butter and briefly fry, butter-side down, in a frying pan or griddle pan. Heat the sesame oil in a separate frying pan. Remove the steak strips from the teriyaki sauce with a slotted spoon, briefly drain, and then fry over a medium to high heat for about 2 minutes on each side. Pour the marinade left in the dish over the meat, bring to the boil and let the steak simmer over a low heat for about 1 minute.

Spread the cut sides of the rolls with a little sweet chilli sauce. Top the bottom halves with a Chinese cabbage leaf and the steak strips. Scatter over the spring onion rings, diced pepper and sesame seeds and place the upper halves on top. Serve immediately.

Sunset in
DOMINO PARK

Urban living shows its sweeter side in *Williamsburg* where a park has been created on the site of the old Domino Sugar refinery, which produced sugar from 1856 to 2004 (at times providing 98 per cent of America's total consumption!). Having opened in 2018, the park now embodies the city's new approach to its waterfronts. You can go for a stroll, enjoy leisure activities or simply sit in the shadow of the *Williamsburg Bridge* and gaze across the *East River* towards the *Lower East Side*. A perfect place for a hot date!

SPICY BURRITOS WITH BEEF, AVOCADO AND BEANS

Wash the tomatoes, remove the stalks and cut into cubes. Wash the chilli, remove the seeds and chop finely. Peel the onion and garlic and cut into small cubes. Pour the kidney beans and sweetcorn into a sieve (fine-mesh strainer) and drain well.

Halve the avocados, remove the stone, scoop the flesh into a bowl and immediately add the lime juice and olive oil. Mash with a fork, add the chilli flakes and season to taste with salt and pepper.

Heat the rapeseed oil in a frying pan (skillet) and fry the minced beef over a medium to high heat for a few minutes, breaking up any lumps of meat with a spoon. Reduce the heat, add the onion, garlic and chilli, and sweat for a few minutes, stirring continuously. Mix in the tomato purée and fry briefly, then deglaze with the stock. Add the tomatoes and simmer, uncovered, for about 10 minutes. Season with salt, pepper and sugar, before stirring in the beans and sweetcorn and heating them through.

Warm a separate frying pan and heat the tortillas one at a time. Spoon a quarter of the grated Cheddar down the middle of each tortilla in a line about 4 cm (1½ in) wide and briefly melt, leaving a border of about 3 cm (1¼ in) around the edges. Don't heat the tortillas for more than about 3 minutes or they will become hard and difficult to roll up.

Meanwhile, wash the lettuce leaves, spin dry and shred. Spoon a quarter of the beef mixture over the cheese on each hot tortilla and spread a little guacamole on top. Scatter over the lettuce. Fold the short side of one tortilla up over the filling and one long side over it, then roll up tightly, leaving the top open. Repeat with the other tortillas to make four burritos. Serve immediately.

MAKES 4

- 2 large tomatoes
- 1 red chilli
- 1 onion
- 1 garlic clove
- 100 g (3½ oz/½ cup) tinned red kidney beans
- 100 g (3½ oz/½ cup) tinned sweetcorn (whole kernel corn)
- 2 large ripe avocados
- juice of 1 lime
- 2 tablespoons olive oil
- ¼ teaspoon chilli (hot pepper) flakes
- 1 tablespoon rapeseed (canola) oil
- 250 g (9 oz) minced (ground) beef
- 2 tablespoons tomato purée (paste)
- about 100 ml (3½ fl oz/scant ½ cup) beef stock
- pinch of sugar
- salt, pepper

OTHER INGREDIENTS
- 4 wheat tortillas
- 120 g (4 oz/1 cup) grated (shredded) Cheddar
- 4 cos (romaine) lettuce leaves

WATERMELON LEMONADE

Bring the sugar with 75 ml (2½ fl oz/5 tablespoons) water to the boil in a small saucepan, stirring continuously. Simmer briefly until the sugar has dissolved, then remove from the heat and leave the syrup to cool.

Cut the watermelon into quarters and peel. Roughly chop the flesh (you should have about 850 g/1 lb 14 oz). Blend to a purée in a food processor, then pass through a sieve (fine-mesh strainer). Halve the limes and juice.

Stir the mineral water, melon purée, lime juice and cooled syrup together in a large jug. Sweeten the lemonade to taste with a little honey and chill for 1 hour.

Rinse the basil and pat dry. Add a few ice cubes to each glass, pour over the lemonade, top with a sprig of basil and serve immediately.

MAKES ABOUT 1.5 LITRES
(51 FL OZ/6⅓ CUPS)
Six 250 ml (8½ fl oz/1 cup)
  glasses
75 g (2½ oz/⅓ cup) sugar
½ watermelon
  (about 1.5 kg/3¼ lb)
4 small limes
500 ml (17 fl oz/2 cups)
  sparkling mineral water

OTHER INGREDIENTS
1–2 tablespoons honey,
  to taste
6 sprigs of basil
ice cubes

MANGO GINGER SMOOTHIES

SERVES 4–6

2 ripe mangoes
200 g (7 oz) ripe pineapple
   (peeled weight)
½ cucumber
1 lime
3 oranges
1 piece of fresh ginger (about
   2 cm/¾ in)
100 ml (3½ fl oz/scant ½ cup)
   sparkling mineral water
300 g (10½ oz/scant 1¼ cups)
   plain yoghurt (3.5 per cent fat)

OTHER
ice cubes
honey, to taste
1 organic lime

Peel the mangoes, cut the flesh away from the stone and dice. Cut the pineapple flesh into similar sized cubes. Peel the cucumber and cut into small pieces. Cut the lime and oranges in half and juice. Peel the ginger and grate finely.

Put all the prepared ingredients in a blender, add the mineral water, yoghurt and a few ice cubes and blend at high speed until smooth and creamy. Depending on the sweetness of the fruit, add a little honey if necessary and blend again before passing through a sieve (fine-mesh strainer).

Wash the lime in warm water, pat dry and slice. Put two ice cubes in each glass and pour over the smoothie. Decorate each glass with a slice of lime and serve immediately.

Springtime
LOVE

Springtime in New York is often short and unpredictable, just like so many love stories. New Yorkers love watching the arrival of spring and seeing the natural world wake up from the hard winter months. First comes the dogwood, followed by the magnolias and cherry blossom. What could be more romantic?

Central Park is in bloom, brides and grooms pose for photographs on *Bow Bridge* or by *Bethesda Fountain*, and you can escape the hustle and bustle of the city in a rowing boat made for two on the *Great Lake* surrounded by the first signs of spring.

Central Park is not the only place bursting with pink blossom: the handkerchief-sized front gardens of *Greenwich Village* and the green central reservation separating the uptown and downtown lanes on *Park Avenue* might also tempt you to take a romantic stroll in nature!

WILD BERRY DALGONA MATCHA

MAKES FOUR 250 ML (8½ FL OZ/1 CUP) GLASSES

150 g (5 oz/1 cup) frozen blueberries
150 g (5 oz/1 cup) frozen raspberries
60 g (2 oz/4 tablespoons) yoghurt
400 ml (13 fl oz/generous 1½ cups) cold milk
4 ice cubes
250 ml (8½ fl oz/1 cup) double (heavy) cream
3 teaspoons sugar
3 teaspoons matcha powder
½ teaspoon vanilla extract

Tip the berries into a blender and allow to thaw. Add the yoghurt and process to a purée, gradually adding enough water until you have a thick smoothie. Transfer to a jug.

Blend the milk with the ice cubes. Whip the cream, sugar, matcha powder and vanilla extract to stiff peaks in a bowl.

Layer the three mixtures into the glasses: first, the berry smoothie, followed by the milk foam, and finishing with spoonfuls of the matcha cream until the glasses are full.

You need to look twice to see New York's small, hidden cafés and restaurants. They are perfect for whiling away romantic hours with your loved one and enjoying all kinds of sweet and indulgent temptations.

SWEET BIG APPLE

SEX AND THE CITY

Finding the love of your life among the millions of New Yorkers is like picking out all the right lottery numbers. No television series illustrates this better than *Sex and the City*. Everything in the series revolves around journalist Carrie Bradshaw (SARAH JESSICA PARKER) and her single, thirty-something friends Samantha Jones, Miranda Hobbes and Charlotte York.

The charming Carrie describes the love lives of New Yorkers in her *Sex and the City* column and her research, and ongoing hunt for Mr Right, throws her and her friends into the hurly-burly of the dating scene. The four women could not be more different: while stylish Carrie is just as interested in the latest Manolo Blahniks as she is in men, tracking down a husband to grow old with is almost an obsession for romantic Charlotte. Love and sex are minor concerns for successful lawyer Miranda, however, whereas Samantha thinks romance is wholly overrated and is always up for a new illicit liaison.

The friends meet up regularly in fancy restaurants, hip bars and legendary nightclubs to sip Cosmopolitans (*see recipe on page 166*) and spill the beans about their amorous adventures, the latest fashion trends and New York gossip.

The mysterious 'Mr Big', whom Carrie encounters in the opening episode, plays a key role in her love life. Their paths continually cross

The architecture on the Upper East Side is reminiscent of Carrie's apartment, which is actually located at 66 Perry Street, between West 4th Street and Bleecker Street in the West Village.

by chance until they end up going out together. Carrie falls in love with him but is uncertain if Mr Big feels the same, so they begin an on-off relationship, loving, fighting and making up until they end up at the altar. Will he get cold feet now things have finally become serious?

FROSTED RED VELVET CAKE

MAKES ONE 20 CM (8 IN) LAYER CAKE

FOR THE BATTER
4 extra large eggs
100 ml (3½ fl oz/scant ½ cup)
 buttermilk
1 teaspoon white wine vinegar
280 g (10 oz/1¼ cups) caster
 (superfine) sugar
30 g (1 oz) unsalted butter
170 g (6 oz/1⅓ cups) plain
 (all-purpose) flour
30 g (1 oz) beetroot (beet) powder
 (from health food stores)
1 teaspoon baking powder
pinch of salt

**FOR THE BISCUIT (COOKIE) CRUMB
COATING**
60 g (2 oz) digestive biscuits
 (graham crackers)
20 g (¾ oz/scant ¼ cup) ground
 hazelnuts (filberts)
1 tablespoon brown sugar
pinch of sea salt
40 g (1½ oz) unsalted butter

FOR THE CREAM CHEESE ICING
400 g (14 oz/1¾ cups) full (whole)
 fat cream cheese (at room
 temperature)
200 g (7 oz/scant 1 cup) unsalted
 butter, softened
½ teaspoon vanilla extract
150 g (5 oz/1¼ cups) icing
 (confectioner's) sugar (sifted)

OTHER INGREDIENTS
unsalted butter and flour, for
 preparing the tins (pans)

Preheat the oven to 150°C (300°F/gas 1). Grease two 20 cm (8 in) springform cake tins (pans) with butter, dust with flour and, ideally, line the bases with baking parchment as well.

To make the batter, separate the eggs and mix the buttermilk and vinegar together. Whisk the egg yolks with the sugar for 2–3 minutes, then add the buttermilk and vinegar and continue whisking for about 8 minutes until the mixture is pale and leaves a thick trail when the beaters of the whisk are lifted. Melt the butter, allow to cool and fold in. Sift in the flour, beetroot powder, baking powder and salt and fold in until just combined. Whisk the egg whites to stiff peaks and gently fold in without deflating the mixture.

Divide the batter equally between the prepared cake tins and bake, one at a time, in the preheated oven for 30–35 minutes. The cakes are ready when a skewer inserted into the middle comes out clean. Allow to cool, then turn the cakes out onto a wire rack to cool completely.

To make the biscuit crumb coating, increase the oven temperature to 170°C (340°F/gas 3) and line a baking tray (pan) with baking parchment. Finely crush the biscuits in a freezer bag with a rolling pin, tip the crumbs into a bowl and stir in the ground hazelnuts, sugar and salt. Melt the butter, stir into the biscuit mixture and work it with your fingers until the butter coats the crumb mixture. Spread it out on the baking tray and bake in the preheated oven for about 8 minutes.

To make the cream cheese icing (frosting), stir the cream cheese, butter and vanilla together in a bowl until smooth. Gradually stir in the sifted icing sugar, then chill for at least 20 minutes.

Place one cake on a serving plate, with its slightly domed top facing down, and spread the top with icing. Place the second cake on top, flat side down, and spread the top with icing. Spread the remaining icing around the sides of the cake and press the crumb coating all over.

Red Velvet Cake was a speciality of the Waldorf Astoria Hotel in New York in the 1920s, and it's now a top seller in cupcake form at the Magnolia Bakery in Greenwich Village.

CHOCOLATE MOUSSE CAKE

Preheat the oven to 180°C (350°F/gas 4). Line the base of a 20 cm (8 in) springform cake tin (pan) with baking parchment and grease the sides with butter.

To make the base, grind the biscuits to fine crumbs in a food processor. Melt the butter in a small saucepan, add to the crumbs with the salt and process to mix. Press the crumbs firmly over the base of the prepared springform tin in an even layer and bake in the preheated oven for about 8 minutes. Leave to cool in the tin.

To make the chocolate mousse, melt both types of chocolate in a bowl over a bain-marie. Remove the bowl from the heat and stir the cream cheese into the melted chocolates. Whip the cream to stiff peaks. Whisk the eggs with 6 tablespoons of water and the sugar in a heatproof bowl over a bain-marie for about 6 minutes until thick and creamy, making sure the temperature of the mixture does not exceed 65°C (150°F).

Meanwhile, soak the gelatine for 5 minutes in cold water until softened. Squeeze the sheets to remove excess water and stir into the whisked egg mixture until dissolved. Fold in the chocolate mixture and allow to cool briefly before folding in the whipped cream. Cover and chill for 20 minutes. Spread the mousse in an even layer over the biscuit base and chill for at least 6 hours, or ideally overnight, until set.

Leave the cake in the tin until just before serving. To demould it, run a very thin, sharp knife around the edge of the cake and release the spring clip. Remove the cake from the base and carefully transfer to a serving plate. Melt the dark chocolate and drizzle over the top of the cake in a lattice pattern. Leave the chocolate to set, then chill the cake until you are ready to cut it into slices.

MAKES ONE 20 CM (8 IN) CAKE

FOR THE BASE
120 g (4¼ oz) chocolate shortbread biscuits (cookies)
60 g (2 oz) unsalted butter
generous pinch of salt

FOR THE CHOCOLATE MOUSSE
160 g (5½ oz) milk chocolate
100 g (3½ oz) dark chocolate (at least 60 per cent cocoa solids)
300 g (10½ oz/1⅓ cups) full (whole) fat cream cheese
200 ml (7 fl oz/scant 1 cup) double (heavy) cream
3 eggs
3¼ tablespoons caster (superfine) sugar
4 sheets gelatine (gelatin)

OTHER INGREDIENTS
unsalted butter, for greasing the cake tin (pan)
50 g (1¼ oz) dark chocolate (at least 60 per cent cocoa solids)

SWEET BIG APPLE *Sweets & Cakes*

RASPBERRY CRUMBLE BLONDIES

MAKES 16–20

FOR THE CRUMBLE MIXTURE
100 g (3½ oz) cold unsalted butter,
    diced, extra for greasing the tin
75 g (2½ oz/⅓ cup) sugar
150 g (5 oz/1¼ cups) plain
    (all-purpose) flour

FOR THE BLONDIE BATTER
200 g (7 oz) white chocolate
100 ml (3½ fl oz/scant ½ cup)
    double (heavy) cream
150 g (5 oz) unsalted butter, diced
325 g (11 oz/2½ cups) plain
    (all-purpose) flour
2 teaspoons baking powder
pinch of salt
3 eggs
125 g (4 oz/generous ½ cup) sugar
100 g (3½ oz/⅔ cup) chopped
    almonds

FOR THE CREAM LAYER
400 g (14 oz/2 cups) quark
    (20 per cent fat)
2 tablespoons sugar
1 packet (2 teaspoons/8 g)
    bourbon vanilla sugar
1 egg
1 egg yolk
1 teaspoon finely grated organic
    lemon zest
1½ tablespoons cornflour
    (cornstarch), sifted
180 g (6 oz/1¼ cups) fresh
    raspberries

To make the crumble mixture, rub the butter, sugar and flour together in a bowl with your fingertips until it resembles breadcrumbs and reserve.

Preheat the oven to 175°C (340°F/gas 3). Grease a rectangular baking tin (pan), measuring about 22 × 34 cm (9 × 13 in), with butter and line with baking parchment, leaving the parchment overhanging the sides. To make the blondie batter, chop the chocolate coarsely, then melt in a bowl over a bain-marie with the cream and butter, stirring occasionally until smooth. Allow the chocolate mixture to cool slightly while you sift the flour, baking powder and salt into a bowl. Beat the eggs and sugar together in another bowl until thick and creamy, then alternately stir in the flour and chocolate mixtures. Fold in the almonds, spoon the batter into the tin, smooth the top and bake in the preheated oven for about 15 minutes. Leave the oven switched on.

Meanwhile, make the cream layer. Mix the quark, sugar, vanilla sugar, egg, egg yolk, lemon zest and cornflour together in a bowl. Pick through the raspberries, wash them and pat dry if necessary. Remove the tin from the oven and spread over the cream in a thin, even layer. Press the raspberries into the cream and sprinkle the crumble mixture on top. Return the tin to the oven and bake for about 35 minutes until golden brown and a knife or skewer inserted into the middle comes out clean. If the blondies still seem a bit moist, leave them in the turned-off oven for 5 minutes.

Once the blondies have cooled completely, remove them from the tin, discard the baking parchment and cut into squares.

SWEET POTATO TARTLETS

Grease six to seven 10 cm (4 in) tartlet tins (patty pans) with butter and dust with flour, tapping out any excess. To make the dough, mix the flour, cocoa powder, sugar and salt together in a bowl. Cut the butter into small pieces and rub into the flour mixture until it resembles breadcrumbs. Add 3–5 teaspoons of cold water and mix to make a smooth dough. Roll out the dough on a lightly floured work surface, until it is about 4 mm (⅛ in) thick, and line the tins. Press the dough down over the base and up the sides of each tin, trimming away any excess around the top. Prick the bases several times with a fork and chill for about 30 minutes.

Meanwhile, peel the sweet potatoes, cut into pieces and bring to the boil in a small saucepan with the orange juice, 1 tablespoon of water and the butter. Immediately turn the heat down to low, cover and cook for about 20 minutes until the sweet potatoes are soft, stirring frequently. Make sure they do not burn — you can add a little more water if necessary. Transfer the sweet potato to a high-sided container and, using a hand-held blender, process to a purée. Leave to cool.

Preheat the oven to 200°C (400°F/gas 6) and bake the tartlet cases blind for about 8 minutes. Remove the cases from the oven and leave them to cool. Reduce the oven temperature to 180°C (350°F/gas 4).

To make the filling, whisk the cream, egg, egg yolk and sugar together in a bowl until frothy, then stir in the puréed sweet potato, honey (to taste), cream cheese, cinnamon and nutmeg until smooth. Pour the filling into the pastry cases, filling them almost to the top, and bake for 20–22 minutes until the filling is just set. Leave the tartlets to cool completely before removing from the tins. Sprinkle with cinnamon sugar before serving.

MAKES 6–7 TARTLETS
(depending on the depth of the tartlet tins/patty pans)

FOR THE DOUGH
225 g (8 oz/1¾ cups) plain (all-purpose) flour
2 teaspoons cocoa (unsweetened chocolate) powder
3 teaspoons sugar
pinch of salt
125 g (4 oz) cold unsalted butter

FOR THE FILLING
225 g (8 oz) sweet potatoes (unpeeled weight)
2 tablespoons orange juice
1 teaspoon unsalted butter
55 ml (2 fl oz/¼ cup) double (heavy) cream
1 large egg
1 large egg yolk
55 g (2 oz/¼ cup) sugar
2 teaspoons honey (or to taste)
40 g (1½ oz) full (whole) fat cream cheese
½ teaspoon ground cinnamon
pinch of freshly grated nutmeg

OTHER INGREDIENTS
unsalted butter and flour, for preparing the tartlet tins
flour, for dusting
cinnamon sugar, for dusting

KEY LIME PIE

MAKES ONE 22–24 CM (9–10 IN) PIE

FOR THE BASE

200 g (7 oz) digestive biscuits
  (graham crackers)
35 g (1¼ oz/ ⅓ cup) ground
  almonds (almond meal)
pinch of salt
100 g (3½ oz) unsalted butter

FOR THE FILLING

4–5 organic limes
4 large eggs
375 g (13 oz) tinned sweetened
  condensed milk
pinch of salt
100 g (3½ oz/ ½ cup) sugar

To make the base, grind the biscuits into fine crumbs in a food processor or crush them very finely in a freezer bag using a rolling pin. Transfer the crumbs to a bowl and mix in the ground almonds and salt. Melt the butter in a saucepan and stir into the crumb mixture. Press the mixture evenly over the base and sides of a 22–24 cm (9–10 in) non-stick tart tin (pan) with a removable base. Cover and chill for at least 45 minutes.

Preheat the oven to 180°C (350°F/gas 4). To make the filling, wash 1 of the limes in warm water, pat dry and finely grate the zest. Cut all the limes in half and juice. You will need 150 ml (5 fl oz/scant ⅔ cup) juice. Separate the eggs. Whisk the egg yolks and condensed milk together in a bowl on slow speed until smooth, then slowly stir in the lime juice and zest. Do not stir too briskly as you don't want to incorporate air bubbles. Pour the egg yolk mixture into the tin over the biscuit base.

Bake in the pre-heated oven for about 20 minutes until the filling has set. Remove from the oven and leave the pie to cool briefly while you make the meringue. Whisk the egg whites with the salt to firm peaks, then gradually whisk in the sugar, a little at a time, and continue whisking until you have a stiff, shiny meringue.

Reduce the oven temperature to 160°C (320°F/gas 2). Lightly spread about half the meringue over the filling in an even layer. Spoon the remaining meringue into a piping bag fitted with a plain nozzle (tip) and pipe even-sized mounds of meringue over the top of the pie, starting at the outside and working towards the middle. Return the pie to the oven and bake for 10–15 minutes until the tips of the meringue mounds are pale golden, making sure they do not become too dark. Switch off the oven, open the door about 10 cm (4 in), and let the pie cool inside for a while, before fully opening the door and leaving the pie in the oven to cool completely. Carefully remove the pie from the tin and place on a serving plate. Keep refrigerated until ready to serve.

SALTED CARAMEL CHEESECAKE

Preheat the oven to 180°C (350°F/gas 4). Line a 20 cm (8 in) springform tin with baking parchment and grease the rim with butter. To make the base, melt the butter in a small saucepan. Grind the biscuits in a food processor to fine crumbs or crush them very finely in a freezer bag with a rolling pin. Transfer the crumbs to a bowl and mix in the cinnamon. Stir in the melted butter, then press in an even layer over the base of the prepared tin. Bake for 8 minutes in the preheated oven. Leave to cool. Reduce the oven temperature to 160°C (320°F/gas 2) and grease the rim of the tin with butter again (this will stop the top of the cheesecake cracking when it bakes).

To make the filling, split open the vanilla pod and scrape out the seeds. Mix the cream cheeses and quark in a bowl until smooth, then add the sugar, vanilla seeds and sifted cornflour. Stir in with the lemon zest and juice and then carefully fold in the cream, egg and egg yolk until combined, but without overmixing. Spread the filling evenly over the base and bake the cheesecake for about 45 minutes. Switch off the oven, keep the oven door closed and let the cheesecake cool for about 30 minutes, then open the oven door slightly (using the handle of a wooden spoon to prop it ajar) and leave to cool for a further 1½ hours. Remove the cheesecake from the oven, leave to cool completely and chill in the tin for at least 6 hours.

To make the caramel sauce, heat the sugar in a saucepan until it melts, then cook until caramelised. Do not allow it to darken too much. As soon as the caramel is light coloured, carefully pour in the cream and simmer for about 5 minutes, stirring continuously, until it is smooth and liquid. Stir in the butter and sea salt and simmer for another 5 minutes. Leave to cool for about 15 minutes so the sauce can thicken a little. Carefully run a very thin, sharp knife between the cheesecake and the tin and undo the clip. Remove the base of the tin and place the cheesecake on a serving plate. Spread the caramel sauce over the cheesecake and decorate as you wish with small pieces of caramel sweets or fudge.

MAKES ONE 20 CM (8 IN) CHEESECAKE

FOR THE BASE

50 g (1¾ oz) unsalted butter
120 g (4¼ oz) caramelised biscuits (for example Lotus Biscoff) or shortbread biscuits (cookies)
¼ teaspoon ground cinnamon

FOR THE FILLING

1 vanilla pod (bean)
200 g (7 oz) full (whole) fat cream cheese
150 g (5 oz/ ⅔ cup) yoghurt cream cheese
150 g (5 oz/ ¾ cup) low-fat quark
100 g (3½ oz/ ½ cup) caster (superfine) sugar
2 tablespoons cornflour (cornstarch)
1 teaspoon finely grated organic lemon zest
1 tablespoon organic lemon juice
125 ml (4 fl oz/ ½ cup) double (heavy) cream
1 egg, lightly beaten
1 egg yolk

FOR THE CARAMEL SAUCE

75 g (2½ oz/ ⅓ cup) caster (superfine) sugar
120 ml (4 fl oz/scant ½ cup) double (heavy) cream
30 g (1 oz) unsalted butter
2 pinches of sea salt

OTHER INGREDIENTS

butter, for greasing the tin (pan)
3 cream caramel toffees (to taste), or fudge, chopped or broken into small pieces

Harry & Sally

'Men and women can't be friends because the sex part always gets in the way', as Harry (BILLY CRYSTAL) opines to Sally (MEG RYAN), whom he gets to know on a long car journey from Chicago to New York. They have both just graduated from university and are seeking their fortunes in the Big Apple.

After a less than harmonious car trip, Harry and Sally part ways at *Washington Square Arch* before bumping into one another by chance at the airport five years later, and they find themselves seated next to each other on the same plane. In the meantime, Sally has got together with Joe and Harry is engaged to Helen. Just as they did before, they feel they have little in common and engage in verbal jousting.

Another five years pass and their paths cross once again in a New York bookshop. Both are newly separated and they agree to have dinner. They spend a lot of time together, enjoying long phone conversations, and they eventually become friends. The scene in *Katz's Delicatessen*, where Sally loudly fakes an orgasm, is unforgettable.

Despite their mutual attraction, they do everything in their power to avoid ending up in bed together in order not to risk their friendship. Instead, they try to set one another up with their best friends, which turns out rather differently from what they had intended.

Sally bursts into tears after a phone call with Joe, her newly engaged ex-boyfriend, Harry comforts her and the inevitable happens – they sleep together. Harry flees the next morning and Sally, deeply hurt by his departure, no longer takes his calls.

Harry wanders aimlessly through New York on New Year's Eve, remembering all his experiences with Sally, and is forced to admit that he loves her. The long-desired happy ending finally comes at a New Year's party.

*The scene in which Sally meets
her girlfriends and announces
her split with Joe was filmed at
the Loeb Boathouse in Central
Park (on the lake).*

BIG APPLE HAND PIES

MAKES 8

FOR THE DOUGH
285 g (10 oz/2¼ cups) plain
    (all-purpose) flour, plus a little
    more if needed
30 g (1 oz) cornflour (cornstarch)
¼ teaspoon baking powder
¼ teaspoon salt
¼ teaspoon ground cinnamon
175 g (6 oz) cold unsalted butter
50 g (1¾ oz/scant ¼ cup) sugar
2 extra large egg yolks

FOR THE FILLING
30 g (1 oz/ ¼ cup) chopped
    hazelnuts
1 teaspoon honey
2 apples (about 250 g /9 oz)
2 teaspoons lemon juice
1 tablespoon unsalted butter
25 g (1 oz) sugar
½ teaspoon cornflour
    (cornstarch)
1 teaspoon ground cinnamon

OTHER INGREDIENTS
flour, for dusting
milk, for brushing
brown sugar, for sprinkling

To make the dough, sift the flour, cornflour, baking powder, salt and cinnamon together into a bowl. Cut the butter into small cubes, then rub it into the dry ingredients until it resembles breadcrumbs. Mix in the sugar. Stir the egg yolks into 2 tablespoons of cold water, then add to the bowl and bring the mixture together with your hands to make a smooth dough. If the dough is too wet, mix in a little more flour. Shape the dough into a ball, flatten it slightly, then wrap in cling film (plastic wrap) and chill for about 30 minutes.

Meanwhile, make the filling. Toast the hazelnuts in a dry frying pan (skillet), mix in the honey and quickly caramelise the nuts. Remove the nuts from the pan and wipe it clean. Peel and quarter the apples, remove the cores and cut into very fine cubes. Place the diced apple in a bowl and stir in the lemon juice. Melt the butter in a saucepan, add the diced apple and sugar and cook for 2 minutes, stirring continuously. Mix the cornflour with 1½ tablespoons of water to make a smooth paste and stir into the pan. Bring to the boil, stirring continuously, and simmer for about 3 minutes. Mix in the cinnamon and toasted hazelnuts, and remove from the heat.

Preheat the oven to 175°C (340°F/gas 3) and line a baking sheet with baking parchment. Roll out the dough on a lightly floured work surface, until 3–4 mm (⅛ in) thick, and, using a heart-shaped pastry cutter or cup (about 10 cm/4 in in diameter), cut out eight shapes. Gather up the dough trimmings and knead lightly until smooth. Roll out again and cut out eight more shapes using the same pastry cutter or cup. Place half the shapes on the prepared baking sheet and spoon 2–3 teaspoons of apple filling into the middle of each, leaving a border all round. Brush the border with water, lay the remaining dough shapes on top and press the edges together with a fork to seal them firmly. Brush the tops of the pies with a little milk and sprinkle with brown sugar. Using a sharp knife, make a few small cuts in the top of each to allow steam to escape during baking.

Bake in the preheated oven for about 25 minutes until golden brown. Allow to cool for at least 20 minutes before serving.

STRACCIATELLA CUPCAKES

To make the batter, finely chop half the chocolate. Break the remaining chocolate into pieces and melt with the butter in a bowl over a bain-marie. Allow to cool briefly.

Preheat the oven to 180°C (350°F/gas 4). Whisk the eggs and sugar together in a bowl until frothy, then whisk in the milk. Sift in the flour, cocoa powder, baking powder and salt, and fold into the whisked egg mixture alternately with the melted chocolate and butter. Do this gently, without overmixing. Finally, fold in the chopped chocolate.

Line a 12-cup muffin tray (pan) with cupcake cases (paper cups) and divide the batter equally between them. Bake the muffins in the preheated oven for about 20 minutes; they are ready when a fine skewer inserted into the middle of a muffin comes out clean. Leave to cool for a few minutes in the tray, then remove to a wire rack and leave to cool completely.

To make the topping, whip the cream and vanilla sugar to firm peaks. Stir the sugar into the mascarpone until smooth, then mix in the grated chocolate. Fold in the cream and chill for 30 minutes. Spoon the topping into a piping bag fitted with a large fluted nozzle (tip) and pipe it on top of the muffins or spread the topping over in a dome shape using a small palette knife.

To decorate, coarsely grate the dark chocolate and sprinkle it over the cupcakes.

MAKES 12

FOR THE BATTER
100 g (3½ oz) milk chocolate
50 g (1¾ oz) unsalted butter, diced
3 large eggs
125 g (4 oz/½ cup) sugar
125 ml (4 fl oz/½ cup) milk
200 g (7 oz/scant 1⅔ cup) plain (cake) flour
3 tablespoons cocoa (unsweetened chocolate) powder
2 teaspoons baking powder
pinch of salt

FOR THE TOPPING
150 ml (5 fl oz/scant ⅔ cup) double (heavy) cream
1 packet (2 teaspoons/8 g) bourbon vanilla sugar
250 g (9 oz) mascarpone
25 g (1 oz) sugar
75 g (2½ oz) grated dark chocolate

FOR DECORATION
20 g (¾ oz) dark chocolate

The city's heart beats a little faster in *Greenwich Village*, *Soho* and *Chelsea*. Not only is it home to the lively LGBTQ+ community (the historic *Stonewall Inn* is located on *Christopher Street*), but all those seeking a moment of togetherness will also find plenty of romantic hideaways, cafés and restaurants here.

DOUBLE CHOCOLATE MUD CAKE

MAKES ONE 24 CM (10 IN) CAKE

FOR THE BATTER

240 g (8½ oz) dark chocolate (at least 60 per cent cocoa solids)

290 g (10 oz) unsalted butter, diced

3 eggs

200 g (7 oz/scant 1 cup) sugar

1 packet (2 teaspoons/8 g) bourbon vanilla sugar

200 g (7 oz/1⅔ cup) plain (all-purpose) flour

50 g (1¾ oz/ ½ cup) ground almonds (almond meal) or hazelnuts

4 tablespoons cocoa (unsweetened chocolate) powder

½ teaspoon baking powder

¼ teaspoon salt

150 ml (5 fl oz/scant ⅔ cup) buttermilk

50 ml (1¾ fl oz/3 tablespoons) milk

FOR THE GANACHE

140 g (5 oz) dark chocolate (at least 60 per cent cocoa solids)

125 ml (4 fl oz/ ½ cup) double (heavy) cream

OTHER INGREDIENTS

unsalted butter and flour, for preparing the tin (pan)

2 handfuls of fresh raspberries or blackberries to decorate cake

To make the batter, preheat the oven to 160°C (320°F/gas 2). Grease a 24 cm (10 in) springform tin (pan) with butter and dust with flour, tapping out any excess.

Break the chocolate into chunks and melt with the butter in a bowl over a bain-marie, stirring until smooth. Leave to cool. Whisk the eggs, sugar and vanilla sugar together in a second bowl for about 5 minutes until thick and creamy, then gradually fold in the cooled, melted chocolate and butter.

Mix the flour, almonds or hazelnuts, cocoa powder, baking powder and salt in another bowl. Stir the buttermilk into the milk in a separate bowl. Gradually fold the dry ingredients and the milk mixture alternately into the egg mixture until everything is well combined, without overmixing.

Pour the batter into the springform tin, smooth the top and bake in the preheated oven for about 1 hour 10 minutes. The cake is ready when a skewer inserted into the middle comes out slightly moist. Allow to cool for 15 minutes before removing from the tin and leaving to cool completely on a wire rack.

To make the ganache, break the chocolate into pieces. Heat the cream in a saucepan and remove from the heat just before it boils. Add the chocolate and stir until melted. Leave for about 30 minutes until the ganache thickens a little. Stir the ganache again and spoon over the cake, spreading it out with a small palette knife. Leave the ganache to set, then decorate the cake as you wish with fresh berries before serving.

BLUEBERRY MUFFINS

Melt the butter in a small saucepan. Wash the lemon in warm water and pat dry before finely grating 1 teaspoon of the zest and squeezing 2 teaspoons of the juice. Rinse the fresh blueberries carefully and pat dry, reserving about 30 g (1 oz) for the topping.

Preheat the oven to 180°C (350°F/gas 4). Mix the butter, milk and crème fraîche together in a bowl until smooth. In a second bowl, whisk the eggs, sugar and vanilla sugar together until foamy. Stir in the butter mixture, lemon zest and juice. Sift the flour, baking powder and salt together, and gently fold in, followed by the butter and egg mixture. Lightly fold in the blueberries as well.

Place the 12 paper muffin cases (cups) in a 12-cup muffin tray (pan) and divide the batter equally between them. Bake the muffins in the preheated oven for 20–25 minutes until golden brown (test they are done by pushing a cocktail stick/toothpick into the middle of a muffin – it should come out clean). Allow to cool a little, then remove from the tray and leave to cool completely.

Put the caster sugar in a small bowl. Push the reserved blueberries through a sieve (fine-mesh strainer), catching the juice in the bowl, and mix with the sugar until smooth. Spread on top of the cooled muffins.

MAKES 12

100 g (3½ oz) unsalted butter

1 organic lemon

220 g (8 oz/scant 1½ cups) fresh blueberries (or frozen blueberries if fresh are unavailable)

125 ml (4 fl oz/ ½ cup) milk

85 g (3 oz/ ⅓ cup) crème fraîche

2 extra large eggs

100 g (3½ oz/ ½ cup) sugar

1 packet (2 teaspoons/8 g) bourbon vanilla sugar

250 g (9 oz/2 cups) plain (cake) flour

2 teaspoons baking powder

pinch of salt

OTHER INGREDIENTS

60 g (2 oz/ ¼ cup) caster (superfine) sugar

SWEET BIG APPLE *Sweets & Cakes*

BANANA BREAD CASHEW BARS

MAKES 12

3 ripe bananas (300–350 g/
   10½–12 oz unpeeled weight)
125 g (4 oz/½ cup) cashew
   butter
50 g (1¾ oz/¼ cup) brown sugar
2 tablespoons honey
150 ml (5 fl oz/scant ⅔ cup)
   cashew non-dairy milk
2 large eggs
250 g (9 oz/2¾ cups) rolled oats
3 tablespoons plain
   (all-purpose) flour
1 teaspoon baking powder
1 teaspoon ground cinnamon
¼ teaspoon salt
100 g (3½ oz/⅔ cup) whole
   cashews
80 g (3 oz/scant ½ cup) chopped
   dark chocolate or chocolate
   chips

OTHER INGREDIENTS

60 g (2 oz/¼ cup) caster
   (superfine) sugar
2 tablespoons cashew non-dairy
   milk

Preheat the oven to 180°C (350°F/gas 4) and line a 25-cm (10-in) square baking tray (pan) with baking parchment. Peel the bananas and mash to a purée in a bowl with a fork. Stir in the cashew butter, sugar, honey and cashew non-dairy milk, mixing thoroughly before beating in the eggs.

Mix the rolled oats, flour, baking powder, cinnamon and salt in a second bowl, then stir into the banana mixture. Finely chop the cashews and mix with the chocolate chunks, then mix into the dough.

Spoon the dough into the prepared tray, smooth the top and bake in the preheated oven for about 30 minutes until golden brown. Allow to cool slightly. Stir the caster sugar into the cashew non-dairy milk and brush a thin layer over the warm cake. Carefully remove the cake from the tray and leave to cool. Cut in half and then into 12 bars of equal size.

PEANUT BUTTER DONUTS

To make the dough, mix the flour, salt, yeast, caster sugar and vanilla sugar together in a bowl. Make a well in the centre and add the diced butter, milk and egg. Mix to make a dough, then knead for about 7 minutes until smooth and elastic. Cover the bowl with cling film (plastic wrap) and let the dough prove for 1–2 hours until it has doubled in volume.

Divide the dough into ten pieces, each weighing about 50 g (1¾ oz). Shape into balls on a lightly floured work surface. Sprinkle the surface with another layer of flour, put the balls on top, cover and leave to prove again for 20 minutes. Push your thumb through the middle of each dough ball to create a hole and make circular movements with your thumb to widen the hole until it is 3–4 cm (1¼–1½ in) in diameter. Cover and leave the dough rings on a floured work surface to prove for another 15 minutes.

Meanwhile, heat 4 cm (1½ in) of oil for deep-frying to about 175°C (340°F) in a large saucepan. Using a large slotted spoon, lower the donuts into the hot oil one at a time and deep-fry in batches until golden brown, turning once. Drain on paper towel and leave to cool completely.

To make the icing, break the chocolate into small pieces and melt with the other ingredients in a bowl over a bain-marie, stirring constantly until smooth. Allow to cool a little, then spread on top of the donuts. Sprinkle the chopped peanuts finely and sprinkle on one side of the icing before it sets. Serve the donuts once the icing has set.

MAKES 10

FOR THE DOUGH
285 g (10 oz/2¼ cups) plain (cake) flour
pinch of salt
2 teaspoons fast-action dried yeast (about 4 g/¼ oz)
25 g (1 oz) caster (superfine) sugar
1 packet (2 teaspoons/8 g) bourbon vanilla sugar
25 g (1 oz) softened unsalted butter, diced
125 ml (4 fl oz/½ cup) lukewarm milk
1 large egg

FOR THE ICING (FROSTING)
100 g (3½ oz) dark chocolate
30 g (1 oz) peanut butter
1 teaspoon caster (superfine) sugar
1 teaspoon coconut oil

OTHER INGREDIENTS
flour, for dusting
1.5 litres (51 fl oz/6⅓ cups) vegetable oil, for deep-frying
40 g (1½ oz/¼ cup) finely chopped peanuts, for sprinkling

SWEET BIG APPLE *Sweets & Cakes*

TRIPLE CHOC COOKIES

MAKES 16

150 g (5 oz/1¼ cups) plain (cake)
  flour

¾ teaspoon baking powder

3 heaped teaspoons cocoa
  (unsweetened chocolate)
  powder

100 g (3½ oz) softened unsalted
  butter, diced

55 g (2 oz/¼ cup) sugar

1 packet (2 teaspoons/8 g)
  bourbon vanilla sugar

1 extra large egg

55 g (2 oz) white chocolate

55 g (2 oz) dark chocolate

55 g (2 oz) milk chocolate

OTHER INGREDIENTS

sea salt, for sprinkling

Sift the flour with the baking powder and cocoa powder into a mixing bowl. Beat the butter with the sugar and vanilla sugar in another bowl until light and creamy. Beat in the egg, then gradually stir in the dry ingredients until combined. Chop the white, dark and milk chocolates and fold in, then chill for 20 minutes.

Preheat the oven to 175°C (340°F/gas 3) and line a baking sheet with baking parchment. Roll the mixture into 16 balls, each about 4 cm (1½ in) in diameter. Place the balls, well spaced apart, on the prepared baking sheet and press to flatten.

Sprinkle the cookies with a little sea salt and bake in the preheated oven for 12–15 minutes. When the cookies come out of the oven, they will still seem quite soft, but will firm up on the baking sheet as they cool.

COOKIES AND CREAM ICE CREAM

Slit open the vanilla pod and scrape out the seeds. Crumble the cookies; the crumbs don't have to be too fine so there can still be some larger lumps.

Mix the milk, condensed milk, vanilla seeds and salt in a bowl. Whisk the cream to stiff peaks. Stir one-third of the cream into the milk mixture, then fold in the remaining cream and the biscuit crumbs. Pour the mixture into an ice-cream machine and churn for about 30 minutes or follow the manufacturer's instructions. Alternatively, pour the mixture into a freezerproof container, filling it to a depth of about 4 cm (1½ in). Cover with a lid and freeze for 4–6 hours, stirring the ice cream well every 30 minutes for the first 2 hours to break up any ice crystals and ensure the ice cream is smooth. After 2 hours, stir every hour until frozen.

Melt the cooking chocolate in a bowl over a bain-marie and spread out the almonds in a shallow bowl. Dip the tops of the ice-cream cones first in the chocolate, then in the almonds and leave to set. Transfer the ice cream to the refrigerator about 10 minutes before serving, so it softens sufficiently to be scooped into the cones. Use an ice-cream scoop, if you have one. Enjoy immediately!

SERVES 4–6

1 vanilla pod (bean)
4 Triple Choc Cookies (see recipe on page 124, or use another chocolate cookie)
150 ml (5 fl oz/scant ⅔ cup) milk
150 g (5 oz) tinned sweetened condensed (evaporated) milk
pinch of salt
200 ml (7 fl oz/scant 1 cup) double (heavy) cream

OTHER INGREDIENTS
50 g (1¾ oz) dark cooking chocolate
30 g (1 oz/scant ¼ cup) chopped almonds
ice cream cones, for serving

As another day draws to an end, it is time for New York's nightlife to wake up in the raft of bars that look out over its breathtaking skyline, hence its reputation as the city that never sleeps.

ON CLOUD NINE

DRINKS & PARTY FOOD

The rooftops of New York are no longer simply home to the city's famous water tanks. More and more residents are discovering that they offer the perfect location for the sort of entertainment that makes life worth living!

The *Metropolitan Museum* has a very special roof garden that boasts a perfect view of *Central Park* and the imposing *Central Park West* building and plays host to a constant stream of art installations at the same time. There's also a bar, of course. Anyone for a Martini sundowner?

FROM THE ROOFTOP

Sleepless in Seattle

Widower Sam Baldwin (TOM HANKS) tells his moving story to millions of radio listeners, so winning the heart of Annie Reed (MEG RYAN) from Baltimore.

Annie takes her fiancé Walter to visit her parents in order to announce their engagement. On the journey home, they hear 8-year-old Jonah on the radio explaining how he really wants to find a new partner for his father, Sam, who is still grieving after losing his wife. The radio presenter then invites a very surprised Sam to go on air and talk about her death and his current life. Sam speaks about his wife and their love in a deeply tender way, explaining how he has been unable to sleep since she died. Days later, Annie is still thinking about the sensitive Sam, but continues to plan her marriage to Walter in New York.

Inspired by the film *An Affair to Remember*, Annie writes a letter to Sam suggesting they meet on the roof of the *Empire State Building* on Valentine's Day. Unbeknownst to Annie, her friend Becky posts the letter.

Jonah is excited by the letter and tries to convince his father to go on the date, but his attention is focused on a new acquaintance by the name of Victoria, whom Jonah cannot stand. Annie flies to Seattle on the pretext of doing research for an article. She sees Sam embracing his sister and thinks he is now spoken for.

Back in Baltimore, Annie receives a letter from Sam (written by Jonah), confirming their date on Valentine's Day. Jonah takes a flight to New York that day and his worried father follows him to the *Empire State Building* observation deck. Annie, who has broken off her engagement, spontaneously also turns up at the agreed meeting place. Annie and Sam meet for the first time and feel an instant attraction as the city's skyline stretches out behind them.

NEGRONI

MAKES 2 DRINKS

60 ml (2 fl oz/ ¼ cup) gin
60 ml (2 fl oz/ ¼ cup) red
vermouth
60 ml (2 fl oz/ ¼ cup) Campari
60 ml (2 fl oz/ ¼ cup) freshly
squeezed blood orange juice

OTHER INGREDIENTS
½ organic orange
ice cubes

Wash the orange in warm water, pat dry and peel two large strips of zest, leaving the bitter white pith behind.

Add four ice cubes to each glass, followed by half the gin, vermouth, Campari and blood orange juice. Stir all the ingredients together for about 30 seconds using a bar spoon until well mixed. Decorate the edge of each glass with a strip of orange zest and then serve the drinks immediately.

SHRIMP SLIDERS

To make the buns, prepare the dough and leave it to prove. Divide the dough into eight equal pieces, about 60 g (2 oz) each, on a lightly floured work surface and roll into balls. Arrange on a baking sheet lined with baking parchment, flatten slightly, then cover and leave to prove for another 20 minutes.

Meanwhile, make the aioli. Peel and crush the garlic, then whisk it in a bowl with the egg yolk, vinegar, sugar and salt. Add the oil, drop by drop to begin with, and then in a thin stream as soon as the aioli thickens. Keep whisking until the aioli is thick and creamy. Season with the lime juice and more salt to taste, then chill until serving.

To bake the buns, preheat the oven to 180°C (350°F/gas 4). Whisk the egg yolk and brush it over the buns, sprinkle with the sesame seeds and bake in the preheated oven for about 20 minutes until golden brown. Leave to cool on a wire rack.

To make the filling, wash the lettuce, spin dry and tear the leaves into pieces that will fit inside the buns. Wash the tomato, remove the stalk and cut into slices. Peel the onion and cut into thin rings. Wash the courgette, slice, then fry in 1 tablespoon of rapeseed oil in a griddle pan for about 5 minutes, turning once. Drizzle with honey and vinegar, season to taste with salt and pepper, remove from the pan and keep warm.

Rinse the shrimp, pat dry and fry in the remaining oil in a frying pan (skillet) over a medium to high heat for 2–4 minutes. Juice the half lime. Season the shrimp with salt, pepper and chilli flakes, to taste, and add the lime juice.

Slice open the buns. Clean the griddle pan, heat a little oil in it and briefly toast the cut sides of the buns, pressing down on them lightly if necessary. Spread aioli on both cut sides and pile lettuce, tomato, courgette and onion on the lower halves of the buns. Place the shrimp on top and replace the bun lids. Secure the burgers with wooden skewers, if you wish, and serve immediately.

MAKES 8

FOR THE BUNS
1 quantity of bun dough (see Hot Dogs with Pickle Relish recipe on page 64)
1 egg yolk, for brushing
8 teaspoons mixed white and black sesame seeds

FOR THE AIOLI
2 garlic cloves
1 egg yolk
1 teaspoon white wine vinegar
1 teaspoon sugar
150 ml (5 fl oz/scant ⅔ cup) rapeseed (canola) oil
squeeze of lime juice
salt

FOR THE BURGERS
1 little gem lettuce
1 large tomato
½ red onion
½ large courgette (zucchini)
50 ml (1¾ fl oz/3 tablespoons) rapeseed (canola) oil
1 teaspoon honey
1 teaspoon white balsamic vinegar
200 g (7 oz) raw shrimp (prawns), peeled and deveined (or frozen shrimp, defrosted)
½ lime
chilli (hot pepper) flakes
salt, pepper

OTHER INGREDIENTS
flour, for dusting
oil, for toasting the buns

ON CLOUD NINE *Drinks & Party Food*

Sunset Time

New York sunsets are amazing! Sunsets can be romantic anywhere, but they have a special magic in this city. The *Statue of Liberty* is a must-see on any trip, of course, even if it's from the deck of the *Staten Island* Ferry – the evening sun turns the view into one of nature's great spectacles.

You can admire the sunset without visiting *New York Harbor*, of course. Enjoy it from the observation decks of the *Rockefeller Center* or the *Empire State Building*, from *Brooklyn Bridge* or the waterfront promenades. The city is full of magic and promise in the golden evening light, a testament to human endeavor, energy and life force.

CHICKEN CURRY SKEWERS

MAKES ABOUT 8 SKEWERS

FOR THE SKEWERS
500 g (1 lb 2oz) boneless chicken
   breast, skinned
50 g (1¾ oz/scant ¼ cup) plain
   yoghurt
2 tablespoons milk
½ organic lime
1 garlic clove
1 piece of fresh ginger (about
   1.5 cm/ ½ in)
2 tablespoons honey
1½ teaspoons curry powder
½ teaspoon ground turmeric
¼ teaspoon ground cumin
¼ teaspoon ground fenugreek
pinch of chilli (hot pepper) flakes
salt, pepper

FOR THE DIP
½ organic lime
1 garlic clove
1 piece of fresh ginger (about
   1.5 cm/ ½ in)
150 g (5 oz/scant ⅔ cup) crème
   fraîche
1 tablespoon honey
1½ teaspoons curry powder
½ teaspoon ground turmeric
pinch of chilli (hot pepper) flakes
50 g (1¾ oz) cream cheese
salt, pepper

OTHER INGREDIENTS
rapeseed (canola) oil, for frying

To make the skewers, rinse the chicken breast, pat dry and slice lengthways into strips about 8 mm (⅓ in) thick. Mix the yoghurt with the milk in a shallow dish. Wash the half lime in warm water, pat dry, then grate (shred) the zest finely and juice. Peel and crush the garlic. Peel the ginger and grate finely.

Stir the lime zest and juice, garlic, ginger, honey and spices into the yoghurt mixture, season generously with salt and pepper and lay the chicken strips in the marinade, making sure they are well coated. Cover and chill for at least 2 hours.

Meanwhile, make the dip. Wash the half lime in warm water, pat dry, grate the zest finely and juice. Peel the garlic and ginger and chop finely. Stir the crème fraîche, lime zest and juice, garlic, ginger, honey, curry powder, turmeric and chilli flakes into the cream cheese in a bowl. Season to taste with salt and pepper and chill until ready to serve.

Lift the chicken strips out of the marinade, letting excess drip back into the dish. Thread about three strips onto a wooden or metal skewer (you'll need eight skewers in total). Heat a little oil in a frying pan (skillet) or griddle pan and fry the skewers on all sides in batches over a medium heat for about 5 minutes until golden brown. Serve with the curry dip.

COLESLAW IN A JAR

Remove and wash the outer leaves of the cabbage. Cut the cabbage in half and in half again, then cut away the triangular wedges of stem. Shred the leaves very finely with a sharp knife. Put the strips of cabbage in a bowl, add salt to taste and toss vigorously with your hands for about 5 minutes until the cabbage softens.

Peel the carrots and shred finely using a mandolin. Peel the onion and dice finely. Rinse the parsley, pat dry, strip the leaves off the stalks and chop finely. Mix the carrots, onion and parsley with the strips of cabbage.

Mix the sour cream, cream, oil, apple vinegar, honey and lemon juice together and season generously with salt and pepper. Toss the dressing with the cabbage mixture, and season again with salt and pepper. Spoon into four 250 ml (8½ fl oz/1 cup) screw-top jars, close and chill for at least 4 hours before serving.

MAKES FOUR SCREW-TOP JARS, EACH ABOUT 250 ML (8½ FL OZ/1 CUP)

½ head of white cabbage (about 850 g/scant 2 lb)
2 carrots (about 200 g/7 oz)
½ onion
6 sprigs of parsley
125 g (4 fl oz/ ½ cup) sour cream
50 ml (1¾ fl oz/3 tablespoons) double (heavy) cream
2 tablespoons rapeseed (canola) oil
1 tablespoon apple vinegar
1½ tablespoons honey
1 teaspoon lemon juice
salt, pepper

Head for the bustling streets, from *Broadway* to the *Blue Note* jazz club. Nighttime New York transforms into an eclectic, diverse, pulsating backdrop for clubbing, dancing or a simple midnight stroll. You are the director of your own film, and the city has space, fun and tolerance for everyone.

CHINATOWN SPRING ROLLS

MAKES ABOUT 20 SMALL ROLLS

20 frozen spring roll wrappers
   (from an Asian supermarket,
   online or a large supermarket)
2 spring onions (scallions)
2 carrots
75 g (2½ oz/generous ¾ cup)
   beansprouts (from a jar)
1 piece of fresh ginger (about
   2 cm/¾ in)
200 g (7 oz) minced (ground)
   pork
1 tablespoon rapeseed (canola)
   oil
80 g (3 oz) cellophane noodles
1½ tablespoons soy sauce
salt, pepper

OTHER INGREDIENTS
oil, for frying
sweet chilli sauce, for dipping

Defrost the spring roll wrappers. Wash the spring onions and slice very finely into rings. Reserve a few for garnish. Peel the carrots and shred finely with a mandolin. Rinse the beansprouts in a sieve (fine-mesh strainer) and leave to drain. Peel the ginger and grate (shred) finely. Fry the minced pork in the oil in a large frying pan (skillet) over a medium heat, breaking up any lumps of meat with a spoon. Add the spring onions, carrots, beansprouts and ginger and fry over a low heat for 2 minutes.

Cook the cellophane noodles according to the instructions on the packet. Drain, rinse in cold water, snip into short lengths with scissors and stir into the meat mixture. Season with the soy sauce and salt and pepper, to taste.

Place one spring roll wrapper on a dish towel and brush the edges with a little water. Spoon about 1 tablespoon of filling onto the wrapper, leaving the bottom third of it clear. Fold this over the filling, fold in the sides and roll up from the bottom. Repeat with the remaining wrappers and filling to make about 20 rolls.

Heat about 3 cm (1¼ in) of oil in a large saucepan to about 175°C (340°F) and fry the spring rolls in batches until golden brown, turning several times so they colour evenly. Drain and leave to dry on paper towel. Garnish with the reserved spring onion slices and serve with a bowl of sweet chilli sauce for dipping.

Top tip: For a veggie option, replace the minced pork with 100 g (3½ oz) shredded Chinese leaves (Napa cabbage) and 50 g (1¾ oz/⅓ cup) chopped cashews.

SAKE MOJITOS
WITH GINGER

MAKES 4 DRINKS

1 bunch of mint
2 large organic limes
1 piece of fresh ginger (about 2 cm/ ¾ in)
8 teaspoons Demerara sugar
400 ml (13½ fl oz/generous 1½ cups) sake (Japanese
rice wine)
300 ml (10 fl oz/1¼ cups) sparkling mineral water

OTHER INGREDIENTS
crushed ice
sprigs of mint, for garnishing

Rinse the mint, pat dry and strip the leaves off the stalks.
Wash the limes in warm water, pat dry and cut into 2 cm (¾ in) pieces.
Peel the ginger and grate finely.

Divide the pieces of lime and the ginger between four glasses and add
2 teaspoons of sugar and a handful of mint leaves to each. Muddle the
limes and mint leaves with the handle of a wooden spoon.

Half-fill the glasses with crushed ice, then pour 100 ml (3½ fl oz/scant
½ cup) sake and 75 ml (2½ fl oz/5 tablespoons) mineral water into
each. Stir once, garnish with mint sprigs and serve immediately.

THE
GREAT
GATSBY

Wild parties with dazzling guests, jazz and endless drinks: F Scott Fitzgerald's novel has been filmed a number of times and provides a telling portrait of the Roaring Twenties in the fictitious town of West Egg on *Long Island*, at the southern tip of New York State. It recounts the story of the mysterious Jay Gatsby from the perspective of narrator Nick Carraway, a young man who has moved to Long Island to try his luck as a bond trader on Wall Street. Millionaire Jay Gatsby, whose origins are mysterious and whose vast fortune has given rise to all kinds of speculation, lives in the luxury villa next door. He holds riotous, lavish parties for New York society on his estate and regularly invites Nick, who is fascinated by the glamour and extragavance but does not grasp the extent of Jay's loneliness.

Jay has unhappily fallen in love with the beautiful Daisy Buchanan, who married Tom Buchanan while Gatsby was away in the army. Nick and a friend of Daisy's try to bring about a reunion between Daisy and Jay, and she is torn between her feelings for her husband and for Gatsby. A group outing by the main characters to *The Plaza* hotel in New York opens Tom's eyes to the danger that he may lose his wife to Jay. Punches are thrown and both lay claim to Daisy's love. Tom is furious and ultimately sends Daisy and Jay home.

Daisy is at the wheel on the journey back when Myrtle Wilson, Tom's lover, runs in front of the car, is run over and dies soon after. Filled with panic, Daisy drives off. Tom hints to the dead woman's husband that the car causing the accident belonged to Gatsby, and Wilson shoots and kills Jay the morning after the accident, before taking his own life.

Alongside Nick, the only people to attend the funeral of the Great Gatsby are Jay's father and a nameless stranger. New York high society has lost all interest in him and even Daisy fails to pay him this last respect. Gatsby's dream of everlasting love is ultimately denied.

ENCHILADA CUPS

MAKES 12 CUPS

FOR THE FILLING
1 red onion
1 green (bell) pepper
1 yellow (bell) pepper
2 tomatoes
1 tablespoon olive oil
75 g (2½ oz) lardons
250 g (9 oz) minced (ground) pork
2 tablespoons tomato purée
75 ml (2½ fl oz/5 tablespoons)
   Mexican enchilada sauce (or
   salsa sauce)
125 g (4 oz) tinned black beans
   or pinto beans
125 g (4 oz/1 cup) grated
   (shredded) cheese
salt
sugar

FOR THE TOPPING
½ little gem lettuce
½ small lime
50 ml (1¾ fl oz/3 tablespoons)
   olive oil
2 sprigs of coriander (cilantro)
   leaves
60 g (2 oz/¼ cup) crème fraîche
salt, pepper
sugar

OTHER INGREDIENTS
6 tortillas, about 22 cm (9 in)
   in diameter

To make the filling, peel the onion and chop finely. Wash the peppers, halve, remove the seeds and membrane and cut into small cubes. Wash the tomatoes, remove the stalks and then cut into small cubes. Heat the olive oil in a large frying pan (skillet), add the onion and sweat briefly before adding the peppers and frying over a medium heat for about 5 minutes. Remove the onion, pepper and tomatoes from the pan and reserve.

Add the lardons to the pan and fry over a medium heat until browned. Add the minced pork and fry for a few minutes, breaking up any lumps of meat with a spoon. Stir in the tomato purée and fry briefly, before deglazing with the enchilada sauce and mixing in the tomato, pepper and onion mixture. Rinse the beans in a sieve (fine-mesh strainer), drain, and mix in as well. Simmer over a low to medium heat for 5 minutes and then season to taste with salt and sugar.

Meanwhile, preheat the oven to 180°C (350°F/gas 4). Cut the tortillas in half and use them to line a 12-cup muffin tray (pan), shaping the halves into cups and pressing them down carefully into the base of each muffin cup. Take care not to tear the tortillas as you do this. Fill each cup with 2–3 tablespoons of the pork mixture and sprinkle the grated cheese on top. Bake in the preheated oven for about 10 minutes.

While the tortillas are baking, wash the lettuce, spin dry and shred finely. Squeeze the half lime and mix the juice with the olive oil and some salt, pepper and sugar. Rinse the coriander, pat dry, strip the leaves off the stalks and chop finely. Toss the lettuce and coriander with a little of the dressing. Lift the hot enchilada cups carefully out of the muffin tray, top with the lettuce mixture and add a spoonful of crème fraîche. Drizzle with the remaining dressing and serve.

Tip: For a vegetarian option, omit the lardons and minced pork and replace them with tinned sweetcorn (whole kernel corn).

CAPRESE SOUP SHOTS

To make the soup, cut a cross in the base of each tomato, immerse briefly in boiling water, then cool in cold water, peel off the skins and deseed. Remove the stalks and, using a blender (or a hand-held blender), process to a purée with the olive oil, tomato juice, tomato purée, balsamic vinegar, oregano, 1 teaspoon of sugar and a little salt and pepper. If the soup is too thick, thin with a little water. Season to taste with sugar, salt and pepper, and chill until ready to serve.

To make the mozzarella foam, cut the mozzarella into small cubes. Heat the cream in a small saucepan, add the mozzarella and melt over a low heat, stirring continuously. Remove from the heat, season to taste with salt, pepper and chilli flakes, then leave to cool completely.

To serve, froth the mozzarella cream to a foam with a hand-held blender. Divide the chilled soup between four small glasses or 12 shot glasses and slowly spoon in the foam so it sits on top. Garnish with small sprigs of basil and serve immediately.

MAKES 4 DRINKS OR 12 SHOTS

FOR THE COLD TOMATO SOUP
4 ripe tomatoes
4 tablespoons olive oil
4 tablespoons tomato juice
  (or chopped tomatoes)
2 teaspoons tomato purée (paste)
2 teaspoons balsamic vinegar
1 teaspoon dried oregano
1 teaspoon sugar
salt, pepper

FOR THE MOZZARELLA FOAM
100 g (3½ oz) buffalo mozzarella
  (drained weight)
175 ml (6 fl oz/ ¾ cup) double
  (heavy) cream
salt, pepper and chilli (hot
  pepper) flakes

OTHER INGREDIENTS
small sprigs of basil, for
  garnishing

ON CLOUD NINE *Drinks & Party Food*

COATED NUTS

MAKES 200 G (7 OZ)

200 g (7 oz) unsalted nuts (e.g. cashews
or peanuts)
1 egg white
1 level teaspoon salt
1 level teaspoon sugar
pinch of cayenne pepper
1 teaspoon sweet paprika
½ teaspoon dried oregano
½ teaspoon dried thyme
1 tablespoon grated (shredded) Parmesan

Preheat the oven to 160°C (320°F/gas 2) and line a baking tray (pan) with baking parchment. Spread out the nuts in the tray and roast in the preheated oven for 12–15 minutes until golden. Remove the nuts from the tray and let them cool completely (otherwise the coating will not stick). Leave the oven switched on.

Whisk the egg white to stiff peaks, then whisk in the salt, sugar, spices, herbs and Parmesan. Fold in the cold nuts, ensuring they are well coated with the egg white mixture.

Return the nuts to the lined baking tray, spreading them out so they are not touching. Bake at 160°C (320°F/gas 2) for about 15 minutes until the nuts are golden brown and crispy, turning them over once. Allow to cool.

Tip: Black and green olives go wonderfully with these roasted nuts.

WESTSIDE STORY

Two street gangs clicking their fingers provocatively, Puerto Rican women in swirling dresses, eternal love and ancient grudges, not to mention songs like *America, I Feel Pretty* and *Somewhere*. New York's backyards set the scene for Leonard Bernstein's renowned musical.

Two warring gangs, the white American *Jets* and the Puerto Rican *Sharks*, are engaged in a bitter struggle for control of the streets on the *West Side* of the city.

Riff, leader of the *Jets*, wants to challenge Bernardo, the head of the *Sharks*, and his gang to a fight to resolve the issue. Riff manages to convince his friend Tony to help him and he accompanies him to the dancehall where the two gangs will be that night.

It is there that Tony encounters Maria, Bernardo's sister, and the two immediately fall in love. Bernardo is not happy with this development, however, and brings the lively evening of dancing to an end. While the *Sharks* discuss their new territory on a roof, the *Jets* hold a war council and both gangs agree to meet the following evening for a 'rumble' to settle things. In the meantime, Tony has followed Maria and confessed his love to her on one of the fire escapes that are so typical of New York.

Maria asks Tony to stop the planned rumble and Tony steps in between the two gangs as they face up to each other. Riff pushes Bernardo over, who knifes him in return, sparking a free-for-all that culminates in Tony stabbing Bernardo to death.

Maria learns of her brother's death and rages at Tony, but he is able to convince her that he did not intend to kill Bernardo and they fall into one another's arms, dreaming of a better future in which their love is possible. Further plot twists result in Tony being shot by a *Shark* named Chino and dying in Maria's arms. Both gangs ultimately realise the senselessness of the constant bloodshed and carry Tony's corpse away together.

SESAME CRACKERS
WITH (BELL) PEPPER SALSA

To make the crackers, melt the butter. Mix the flour with the yeast and salt in a bowl. Add the oil, the butter and 85 ml (3 fl oz/⅓ cup) of water and mix to make a dough. Knead for about 7 minutes until the dough is smooth and elastic. Cover the bowl with cling film (plastic wrap) and let the dough prove for about 1½ hours.

Meanwhile, make the salsa. Preheat the oven to 225°C (440°F/gas 8) and line a baking tray (pan) with baking parchment. Wash the peppers, halve and remove the seeds and membrane. Place on the prepared tray, drizzle with the oil and roast in a hot oven for about 25 minutes, turning the peppers occasionally, so the skin blackens and blisters evenly all over. While the peppers are roasting, toast the pine nuts in a dry frying pan (skillet) until golden brown, then leave to cool.

When the peppers come out of the oven, place them in a bowl, cover and leave for about 15 minutes. Peel off their skins, remove the seeds and membrane, chop finely and mix with the pine nuts and ajvar. Add the herbs, then season to taste with salt, pepper, sugar and chilli powder.

Preheat the oven to 200°C (400°F/gas 6) and line two baking sheets with baking parchment. Divide the dough in half and, using a rolling pin, roll each half out as thinly as possible (about 2 mm/⅛ in thick) on a lightly floured work surface. Cut each sheet of dough into about 4 cm (1½ in) squares using a pizza wheel and divide the squares between the prepared baking sheets. Prick each square several times with a cocktail stick (toothpick).

Whisk 1 tablespoon of rapeseed oil with 1 tablespoon of water and brush over the squares, then sprinkle with sea salt and sesame seeds. Bake, one tray at a time, for about 12 minutes until golden brown and crispy. Remove the crackers from the baking sheets to a wire rack and leave to cool before serving with the pepper salsa.

MAKES ABOUT 50 CRACKERS

FOR THE CRACKERS
30 g (1 oz) butter
250 g (9 oz/2 cups) plain
  (all-purpose) flour
½ teaspoon fast-action dried
  yeast
½ teaspoon salt
2 tablespoons rapeseed
  (canola) oil, plus 1 tablespoon
  for brushing

FOR THE SALSA
2 red (bell) peppers
1 yellow (bell) pepper
60 ml (2 fl oz/¼ cup) rapeseed
  (canola) oil
30 g (1 oz/scant ¼ cup) pine nuts
4 teaspoons mild ajvar sauce
  (from a jar)
¼ teaspoon dried oregano
¼ teaspoon dried thyme
salt, pepper, sugar and chilli
  powder

OTHER INGREDIENTS
flour, for dusting
sea salt and sesame seeds,
  for sprinkling

COSMOPOLITAN

MAKES 2 DRINKS

40 ml (2¾ tablespoons) lemon vodka
50 ml (1¾ fl oz/3 tablespoons) cranberry juice
20 ml (1½ tablespoons) Cointreau
4 ice cubes

OTHER INGREDIENTS
2 large organic limes

Wash one of the limes in warm water and pat dry. Cut two long strips
of zest, leaving the bitter white pith behind, and two thin slices of lime
and reserve. Juice both limes; you will need about 20 ml
(1½ tablespoons).

Pour the vodka, cranberry juice, lime juice and Cointreau into a
cocktail shaker, add the ice cubes and shake vigorously.

Pour through a cocktail strainer into two cocktail glasses and decorate
each glass with a strip of zest and a lime slice.

RECIPE LIST

Raspberry Crumble Blondies 96

Frosted Red Velvet Cake 92

Rice
Chicken The Halal Guys' Way 56

Russian Chocolate Coffee Cake 27

S

Sake Mojito with Ginger 151

Salted Caramel Cheesecake 105

Shrimp
Shrimp Sliders 137

Sour Cream
Coleslaw, Preserved 145
Russian Chocolate Coffee Cake 27

Spicy Burritos with Beef, Avocado and Beans 79

Spring Onions
Asian Noodle Boxes 71
Chinatown Spring Rolls 148
Ramen 68
Teriyaki Beef Burgers 72

Spring Roll Sheets
Chinatown Spring Rolls 148

Sweetcorn
Spicy Burritos with Beef, Avocado and Beans 79

Sesame
Granola Berry Bowls 28
Sesame Crackers with Bell Pepper Salsa 165
Teriyaki Beef Burgers 72
Tuna Pretzel Bagels 24
Shrimp Sliders 139

Sesame Crackers with (Bell) Pepper Salsa 165

Sourdough Bread 18

Stracciatella Cupcakes 111

Strawberries
Granola Berry Bowls 28
Vanilla, Cashew and Strawberry Drinks 45

French Toasts Filled with Avocado and Bacon 33

Sugar Snap Peas
Asian Noodle Boxes 71

Sunflower Seeds
Granola Berry Bowls 28

Sweet Potato
Sweet Potato Tartlets 101

Sweet Potato Tartlets 101

T

Teriyaki Beef Burgers 72

Tomatoes
Caprese Soup Shots 159
Chicken The Halal Guys' Way 56
Crêpes-Style Manicotti 63
Deli Pasta Salad 52
Enchilada Cups 154
Pizza Calzone 55
Spicy Burritos with Beef, Avocado and Beans 79
Tuna Pretzel Bagels 24
Shrimp Sliders 137

Tortilla
Enchilada Cups 154
Spicy Burritos with Beef, Avocado and Beans 79

Triple Choc Cookies 124

Tuna
Tuna Pretzel Bagels 24
Tuna Pretzel Bagels 24

V

Vanilla, Cashew and Strawberry Drinks 45

Vermouth
Negroni 134

Vodka
Cosmopolitan 166

W

Watermelon
Watermelon Lemonade 82

Watermelon Lemonade 82

White Cabbage
Coleslaw, Preserved 145
Pastrami Sandwiches 67

Wild Berry Dalgona Matcha 85

Wine
Pizza Calzone 55
Ramen 68
Sake Mojito with Ginger 151

Y

Yoghurt
Chicken Curry Skewers 142
Chicken The Halal Guys' Way 56
Cranberry Breakfast Bread 41
Granola Berry Bowls 28
Mango Ginger Smoothies 81
Pastrami Sandwiches 67
Wild Berry Dalgona Matcha 85

LISA NIESCHLAG

is a designer, cookery author and food photographer with family roots in New York.

Lisa's photographic creations make her many readers hungry for more, particularly when she styles the food in such a mouthwatering way. The kitchen is Lisa's creative and culinary kingdom.

Lisa runs the popular food blog *Liz & Friends*.

www.lizandfriends.de

Mit *Verliebt in New York* setzen die Autoren ihre New-York-Erfolgsreihe fort. Zuvor erschienen im Hölker Verlag:
New York Christmas
New York Christmas Baking
New York Christmas Brunch
New York Capital of Food

LARS WENTRUP

is an all-rounder: designer, illustrator, gourmet, food taster and book lover.

Inspired by Lisa's food styling and photography, Lars creates the perfect layout and brings excellent taste (in every sense) to each book.

Lars has been running a communications design agency in Münster with Lisa since 2001.

www.nieschlag-wentrup.de

JOE THOMAS

Joe Thomas is a travel and architecture photographer from New York City. His spirit of adventure and natural curiosity have taken him to all seven continents to create work.

Joe's work has been appreciated in publications such as *Condé Nast Traveler*, *Travel & Leisure*, the *Washington Post* and the *Boston Globe*.

www.joethomasphoto.com

Photo: Julia Le

A big thank you to Joe Thomas for the many beautiful photos of New York, from which we were able to select the best for this book. Your images capture the essence of the many different faces of the city perfectly. *Thank you*, Joe!

We would also like to thank Christin Geweke for her culinary cooperation, along with Franziska Grünewald and Mareike Bartholomäus for the amazing project support. Thanks to Alexa Nieschlag for the invaluable New York insider tips, and to Andrea Gottfreund for assistence on set. It is only with the help of such a great team that we have been able to create books like these.

Thank you to our dear publishers, Hölker Verlag. We share a great passion for beautiful books.

This edition published in 2023 by Hardie Grant
Books, an imprint of Hardie Grant Publishing.
Original edition © 2022 Hölker Verlag in der
Coppenrath Verlag GmbH & Co. KG, Hafenweg 30,
48155 Münster, Germany. Original title: *Verliebt in
New York. Rezepte und Geschichten*
(ISBN 978-3-88117-272-1)
All rights reserved.

Hardie Grant Books (London)
5th & 6th Floors
52–54 Southwark Street
London SE1 1UN

Hardie Grant Books (Melbourne)
Building 1, 658 Church Street
Richmond, Victoria 3121
hardiegrantbooks.com

In Love with New York
ISBN: 9781784885946
10 9 8 7 6 5 4 3 2
Concept & design: Hölker Verlag
Authors: Lisa Nieschlag und Lars Wentrup
Layout and typesetting: Nieschlag + Wentrup
www.nieschlag-wentrup.de

Illustrations:
Lars Wentrup
Food styling & photography:
Lisa Nieschlag
www.lisanieschlag.de
New York photography:
Joe Thomas
www.joethomasphoto.com
Other images:
picture-alliance/Mary Evans Picture
Library (p. 13), picture-alliance/United
Archives|United Archives/Impress
(p. 30)
Other text: Alexa Nieschlag,
Mareike Bartholomäus
Recipe development: Christin Geweke
Proofreading: Judith Pfeiffer-Ley
Editing: Franziska Grünewald,
Mareike Bartholomäus
Assistant: Andrea Gottfreund
Production: Anja Bergmann
Litho: FSM Premedia GmbH & Co. KG,
Münster, Birgit Depenbrock

Publishing Director: Kajal Mistry
Typesetting: David Meikle
Translation: JMS Books llp and Wendy
Sweetser
Proofreader: Caroline West
Production controller: Sabeena Atchia
Colour reproduction by p2d
Printed and bound in China by Leo
Paper Products Ltd.